Pastoring the Smaller Church

PASTORING the SMALLER CHURCH

JOHN CALDWELL THIESSEN, A. B., B. D.

Late Professor of Missions and Pastoral Theology,
Detroit Bible College, Detroit, Michigan
Author of A Survey of World Missions

ZONDERVAN PUBLISHING HOUSE

OF THE ZONDERVAN CORPORATION | GRAND RAPIDS, MICHIGAN 49506

Pastoring the Smaller Church
Copyright 1962 by
Zondervan Publishing House
Grand Rapids, Michigan

Fourteenth printing   1977
ISBN 0-310-36901-0

Printed in the United States of America

FOREWORD

From time to time a book comes from the press that is a must for every preacher. This latest volume from the pen of the Reverend John C. Thiessen fits into this category.

Since reading the manuscript I have wished many times that someone would have placed a book like this in my hands 25 years ago. At that time I was beginning my ministry and I needed every help I could get. I feel certain that the chapters in this present volume would have done much in enabling me to escape some of the mistakes and pitfalls of the Christian minister to which I fell victim.

Young men preparing for the ministry, young ministers in country or city churches, and all ministers, will be well repaid for reading this book. If its instruction is heeded, I feel certain that we will have churches with congregations spiritually alive doing God's work in God's way.

If anyone reading this foreword is not a minister, purchase this book and give it to your pastor at once. He will thank you for it.

LEHMAN STRAUSS

PREFACE

These lectures were born in the classroom. I was asked to teach pastoral theology, so I looked around for a suitable textbook. I examined a number of books I had in my library on the subject and also in the college library. All of them were good, some better than others. But they all dealt with the large city church. There was practically nothing in them to help the beginner whose first charge was a small church in a small town. So we started out by selecting a number of practical subjects, outlining them and discussing them in class. This continued for several years. Then the outlines were put in more permanent form and the decision was reached to publish them as a book.

There are a few quotations from other writers, but on the whole these notes are based on personal experiences and observations gained through twenty-six years of pastoral work. If I had known these things when I became a pastor, the first few years of my ministry would have been much easier. It is my hope that this book will be of help to beginners in pastoral work and that possibly other pastors of small churches will get help from its pages.

I am deeply grateful to my pastor, Dr. Lehman Strauss, who has written a foreword, after carefully and critically reading the manuscript. I am also thankful to Mrs. William A. BeVier for typing the entire book for the publishers.

With the earnest prayer that God will bless its ministry, this book is sent forth.

JOHN CALDWELL THIESSEN
Detroit, Michigan

TABLE OF CONTENTS

Foreword by Lehman Strauss

Preface

Pastoring the Smaller Church

Chapter 1

THE MEANING AND PURPOSE OF PASTORAL THEOLOGY

The term "Pastoral theology" seems to be somewhat a misnomer. One seeing the words for the first time might get the impression that it was a study of the theological views of a minister of the Gospel. Of course these views are important, but they are usually quite carefully considered when a candidate is being examined for the gospel ministry. In our use of the term, we refer to the entire life and service of a minister of the Lord Jesus Christ.

Perhaps we should explain more fully what we mean. The word "pastoral" indicates that it pertains to a minister in the performance of those duties which distinctively belong to the work of a man in charge of a church. The term "theology" denotes that it pertains chiefly to God and His Word.

Paul's words to Timothy, "Thou shalt be a good minister of Jesus Christ" (1 Timothy 4:6), do not refer to the latter's preaching but to his practical administration of the affairs of the local church of which he was pastor. This is made clear by the context.

It should be remembered that a pastor is no longer a private citizen of the state and community whose responsibilities do not go beyond his own home and his own family: he is a recognized minister of God (I Thessalonians 3:2), and his words and deeds are either a help or a hindrance to the work to which he has been called. The pastor's primary work is preaching, but his life and conduct should be in harmony with what he preaches.

Our present study is designed to be helpful in the work of the ministry outside of the preaching of the Word. *Homiletics* is intended to teach men how to preach; *pastoral theology,* how they ought to deport themselves at all times while filling the office of a pastor. There are things in which members of the church engage but from which the pastor must desist. There are also things the members of the church will not touch but which the pastor must do.

These studies are designed to be helpful to those who are preparing for this work, but they may also be useful to some who are already in a pastorate.

That there is need for such training is taught in the Word, and it also becomes evident when one observes the work of certain pastors. The Lord Jesus certainly prepared the Apostles for their work. For about three years He thoroughly and carefully taught them many things pertaining to success in their ministry of the Gospel — such as seeking first the kingdom of God (Matthew 6:33); being watchful against false teachers (Matthew 7:15, 16); practicing humility (Matthew 18:1-6); disciplining a sinning brother (Matthew 18:15-19); and a great many other things.

This need for instruction and training had not yet ceased in the apostolic period. Three of Paul's letters are commonly called "pastoral epistles" (I and II Timothy, Titus). These three epistles are really a compendium of pastoral theology. It is a mistake to think that if the pastor is genuinely saved and filled with the Holy Spirit he will not need any other training. Certainly Paul did not think so. He instructed Timothy about the duty of prayer on the part of the members of the church; the position and attitude of women; the qualifications of bishops and deacons; the wives of church officials; the care for younger and older widows; and many other things of practical importance (I Timothy 2:1-3, 9-15; 3:1-10, 11; 5:1-16).

The same need exists even to this day. The author had the privilege of studying pastoral theology under a very competent teacher in the seminary, and I greatly profited by what I learned; but in more than twenty-five years of actual work as a pastor, I was confronted with many things I had not anticipated. No instructions regarding them had been given, and there was no one with whom I could counsel; I simply had to wade in and do the work the best I knew how. Often the mistakes I made — and there were many — could have been avoided if I had known then what I know now. I believe the same is true in almost any pastor's experience. However, a careful consideration of the problems of a pastor in advance may often help to avoid pitfalls into which others have fallen.

Sometimes men enter the ministry with no training at all. They have a gift for public speaking and they gather a group of people around them and found a church (usually independent). But their lack of training shows up when the first serious problems arise. More than one such pastor immediately resigns and looks for another church.

Many good books have been written on pastoral theology, but some of these are written almost entirely from a denominational aspect, and practically all of them speak mostly of the large city church and the pastor's relation from the organizational viewpoint. But there are very few such churches available for the man who has just been graduated from Bible college or seminary. If there were, there would be a long waiting list in front of everyone of them. Of course, practically every church has prospects of growth if there is any spiritual life in it, but there are some so located that they can never become large organizations; yet they perform an efficient ministry on a smaller scale. Should these churches be neglected?

For example, in a mid-western state there is a village with about a thousand inhabitants. There are seven churches, one of them Roman Catholic. Within a few miles in the country there are three more Protestant churches. Undoubtedly one of these will be larger and have more influence than the others, but it is hardly likely that any one of them will be a large church like some we find in the cities. Yet there is a place for the small churches and they should have just as competent and thoroughly equipped men as pastors of large churches.

If a church grows large during a man's ministry, he will undoubtedly grow with it and have no need of further specialized training. The ideal preparation would be for a man to serve an "internship" for at least a year under some capable pastor after graduating from school.

Lecturing to students at a theological seminary, a visiting speaker told of having recently delivered a commencement address to a class of graduating nurses. He told them that the proof of their ability would not be seen by working in a modern hospital with all the most recent equipment and with an efficient physician or surgeon at hand. It would be seen in doing a satisfactory job in a small house with only one or two rooms, the patient lying on a bed that was not sanitary, with no oxygen or blood banks available if an emergency should require their use, the doctor delayed in his coming but the expected baby coming on just the same, or the person seriously injured in an accident bleeding to death and needing immediate attention. Similarly, a minister's ability as a pastor is not seen in a large, beautiful, perfectly organized church, where he needs but to lift the finger and the work is done by someone in the organization. It is seen in the hard place — in the one-room church where it is thought a waste of money to employ a janitor; the church where the spiritual life is at a low ebb; the church in which there has been no revival in many years; the church in which there is little or no interest in missions. If he succeeds in such a church, he is indeed a man of God and the one who evidently has the essential qualities to serve as a pastor. And there are more of such churches than there are of their opposite, more than most of us would like to admit.

A capable pastor is one who can go into a strange community, get permission to use the one-room country school house (if any such are left), or some other vacant building, build the fire in the stove, sweep the floor, dust the furniture, invite the people of the community, lead the singing, conduct the services, preach the sermon, deal with inquirers and lead them to Christ, organize a church, and carry on until a real work of the Lord has been established. These and many other things cannot be learned by merely studying the organizational structure of a large city church.

Many excellent books have been written on pastoral theology, and we advise the student to read all he can. But our aim in this book is to discuss many of the things that pertain to a pastor's work from the practical angle in order to help the young minister get a right start. The work is not exhaustive, and some subjects no doubt will be left untouched, but we believe the man who is helped by these discussions will not find additional problems too difficult. He must always remember that he has a great responsibility both Godward and manward, not thinking himself superior to any of his people, but serving the Lord in all humility of spirit, not "as being lords over God's heritage" (I Peter 5:3).

Chapter 2

THE PASTOR'S CALL

What is a call to the ministry? Why do some men believe they have been called to be pastors? How does one receive such a call? We shall deal with these and a few other questions in this chapter.

I. What Is a Pastor?

What is the meaning of the word "pastor"? It is used by most churches to designate the head of a local congregation. It is really the Latin translation of the Greek word *poimen*, which means literally a "herdsman, a shepherd." The word *poimne* means "sheep"; *poimnion*, a "flock of sheep"; *poimaino*, "to feed, to tend a flock, to shepherd the sheep."

The name is fitting because a common designation for believers is that of "sheep." It was so used in the Old Testament of God's people the Jews (Psalm 95:7), and is also the term applied to believers in the New Testament (John 10:3-5, 11, 14, 16; Hebrews 13:20; I Peter 5:2). It is not a very flattering designation, for a sheep is a very ignorant animal in many respects. It is in constant need of the care of a shepherd, and so are also the believers in Christ. Pastoring a church is tending the Lord's flock.

There are two other words used to denote the same ecclesiastical office, namely, *episkopos* (usually translated "bishop"), and *presbyteros* (translated "elder"). Sometimes the word *episkopos* is translated "overseer" (Acts 20:28).

Some denominations believe that there is a distinction between these offices. The *pastor* is the man in charge of a local church; the *elder* (in some cases called *presiding elder*) has a district with a number of churches and pastors under his supervision, or at least could exercise authority in any church of his denomination if difficulties had arisen between a church and its pastor; the *bishop* has the oversight of a large number of districts or conferences. This is roughly the pattern of churches with an episcopal form of government. It is also that of the Roman Catholic church, with many additions. One example is the *College of Cardinals,* from which ranks the pope is chosen. The pope is at the very top and above all the others. He is the supreme authority of the church on earth.

However, a careful study of God's Word shows that the three words refer to the same office. Consider Acts 20:17, 28. In verse 17 we find that the apostle Paul sent for the *elders* of the church at Ephesus. In verse 28 he says that these elders are the *overseers* (*episkopoi*, elsewhere translated "bishops," Philippians 1:1), and then he goes on to say that they are in charge of *the flock*, which makes them pastors, or shepherds. Some churches distinguish between *teaching* elders and *ruling* elders. The pastor is always a teaching elder.

The *elders* are said to have been made bishops (overseers) over the *flock*, with the purpose that they should *feed* ("shepherd," Greek *poimainein*) the church of God. So then the pastor is the elder, the overseer, the one who tends and feeds those under his care. There are three names, but only one office, and a great many functions.

II. WHAT IS A CALL?

Webster's *New Collegiate Dictionary* lists sixteen different meanings of the word. The only one with which we are concerned at the present is the one that says a call "is a summons to a particular duty, office, or employment." In the light of these considerations, we can now form a definition of a call to the pastoral office.

Definition. By a *call to pastoral work* we mean the inner conviction that we have received a divine commission to the preaching of God's Word and such other duties as are associated with it.

The Scriptures teach the necessity of such a call both in the Old Testament and in the New. Prophets, priests, and judges were set apart for their particular office by divine appointment. "And no man taketh this honor unto himself, but he that is called of God as was Aaron" (Hebrews 5:4). The New Testament regards the various orders in the ministry as among the "gifts" which the Holy Spirit has divided among men according to His own will (Ephesians 4:11, 12). It has been said that no man should go into pastoral work if he can possibly stay out of it, *i. e.*, he must feel compelled to say: "Woe is unto me, if I preach not the gospel!" (I Corinthians 9:16).

Preaching is the principal ministry of a pastor. In some circles today this is minimized. It is said the minister must make friends with all the people of the community; he must lead in civic and charitable enterprises; he must labor in behalf of the underprivileged; he must work for the abolition of the many forms of vice such as liquor, gambling, immorality, etc. There is a place for all these, but they are not a pastor's chief function. More will be said about the pastor's relation to the community in another chapter. For the present, we believe the definition is sufficient and Scriptural. It is sufficient because it covers the whole ground. It is Scriptural because the word *pastor* means *shepherd,* and the pastor's first duty is to "feed the flock" (Acts 20:28; I Peter 5:2; also the words of Jesus to Peter at his restoration, John 21:15, 16).

But let us never forget that while preaching is the primary work of the pastor, many other duties fall to his lot, and with these we shall be occupied in these studies.

III. WHY DO SOME MEN BELIEVE THEY ARE CALLED?

Superficial Reasons

We list only a few of these, although a good many more could be added.

1. *Parental pressure.* Sometimes a mother has her heart set on her son's becoming a minister of the Gospel. It could be very wrong if there is nothing more than that. The son may have no qualifications for the high office. The mother's chief ambition may be that her son should become an outstanding man in a community.

However, this may have some bearing on a man's call. Samuel, the last of the judges and the first of the prophets, was dedicated to the Lord before his birth, and even before his conception (I Samuel 1:20-28). Unquestionably Hannah's prayer and vow had much to do with Samuel's becoming the man he was.

In the life story of J. Hudson Taylor we read that his parents had dedicated him to the Lord before he was born.

God may call through a mother's or a father's ambition, but that alone is not enough.

2. *Personal ambition.* There are still some people who think there is a great deal of money in pastoral work, and the pastor never has much to do. What is the basis for such an opinion?

If there is no office or study in the church in which the pastor spends certain hours every day, he will have to do his studying at home. People who call at the home, or have occasion to call him on the telephone, get the impression that he just sits around the house all day. He can sleep as long as he pleases, and when he gets up there is no hard work waiting for him. All he has to do is prepare a couple of sermons for Sunday, and much of the material he uses he gets out of books.

Is this correct? Of course not! But is there not some danger in this direction? The pastor has no boss to outline his work for him or to supervise his activities, or (perish the thought!) drive him to work. He is his own master, and if he is inclined to be lazy he has plenty of opportunity to live according to his inclination. But the true pastor always has plenty to do even in a small church, as we shall see.

As far as his salary is concerned, he may get a decent living out of his salary from the beginning, but there is not much prospect of substantial increases if he stays in a small church. Even in larger churches, the number of pastors who receive as much for the work they do as they would receive for the same amount of secular work is very small.

3. *Preferred service.* Some men enter the ministry because they want to be of service to their fellow men. This may be a very good reason, for pastoral work is an unselfish work for others. But it is not enough. Men and women become teachers, social workers, industrial leaders, sometimes even missionaries for the same reason. The call to the ministry requires more than that.

Significant Reasons

One or all of the following, plus some others, may have a part in a man's call to the ministry.

1. *It is a spiritual ministry.* As a matter of fact, it is the only truly spiritual ministry in the world today. To the mass of men in general, the word "spiritual" does not have a very deep meaning. In political campaigns the leading candidates often talk about spiritual values, powers, and qualities. But what they have in mind is "the intellectual and highest endowments of the mind" (*Webster*). It is really a form of idealism which strives to make improvement in the world as a whole, or in some particular section. Christians use the word with its Scriptural meaning: namely, to denote the inner, invisible, and eternal qualities of a human being, especially in his relation to God. The pastorate, or Christian ministry, is the only calling which is wholly devoted to a service on this level.

2. *It is a ministry which links men with God.* This is really the explanation or expansion of the previous statement. The great end or aim of pastoral work is to help bring about a spiritual union between men and God, and then to help the one thus linked with God to live a life that is pleasing to God. It is a service that will

have eternal results. It is this conviction that enables a man to go on in the ministry in spite of great difficulties and trials.

3. *It conserves all true values for a human being.* This is not true of other professions, such as that of the lawyer or the doctor.

A lawyer is concerned with the civil rights of an individual; so also is the pastor. Very often he is called upon to defend the rights of the friendless in his community. For example, a boy from a certain Sunday school in a large city was falsely accused of indecent exposure, and the word of the pastor's family was helpful in setting him free.

A physician is concerned with the physical health of the patient's body; so also is the pastor. His ministry to the sick is first of all spiritual, but he is also concerned about the patient's health and how it should be conserved, yes, and how lost health may be regained. His words of caution and counsel may often go unheeded, but they may also prove very helpful.

We could go down the line and name anything of true value. The pastor is concerned about conserving *all* these, which is not true of other vocations. The supreme interest of the Christian ministry is in the human soul, and this is essential to the welfare of any human being.

IV. How Does a Pastor Receive His Call?

The apostles received a *personal call* from the Lord Jesus Christ (Luke 6:13). They had been His disciples, or followers, for some time, and one day He called them and commissioned them to be apostles. He was present in person and called them with an audible voice. *We* have never met anyone who received his call in this way. It is impossible today.

The apostle Paul received his call in a *vision* in connection with, or immediately after, his conversion (Acts 9:5). After this he also received a personal message from Ananias to the same effect (Acts 9:15-17; see also Galatians 1:1, 15, 16).

Timothy and Titus received their call through the *apostle Paul* (Acts 16:1-3; II Corinthians 8:16). But it should be noted that God also wrought in the hearts of these two men, especially that of Titus, giving him a personal concern for the Corinthian Christians.

Every Christian should seek God's guidance, and if he keeps his heart and mind open toward God, he will find out whether or not God has called him to the ministry of the Gospel.

Are there any men in pastoral work whom God did not call?

Without a doubt. We can positively identify them by some, or all, of the following traits:

(1) They regard their work as a profession rather than as a distinct call from God. They chose the pastorate like another man might choose teaching, or medicine, or law, or some other professional activity.

(2) They do not consider the winning of souls for Christ as their supreme task. Some do not even believe in the necessity of conversion for one to become a Christian.

(3) They are often men who deny the authority, integrity, and inspiration of the Word of God.

(4) They are usually men who construct their sermons out of what they read in the writings of other men and use the Bible only to find a few words to serve as a suitable text for their message.

(5) They are often men who easily step out of the ministry when they become disillusioned about the nature of the work and the income they receive.

What shall we say in conclusion? Pastoral work is God's work in human hands. Pastoral work is performed by men whom God has called. Pastoral work, along with all true Christian work, is the greatest ministry in the world. Pastoral work will bring eternal rewards.

CHAPTER 3

THE PASTOR'S QUALIFICATIONS

What qualifications should a man have for pastoral work? Does the Lord call only those who have these qualifications? Are these qualifications enough to prove that a man has been called to the ministry regardless of whether he has any training or not? Are they enough to enable him to carry on a successful pastorate? Can anything be done to add to these qualifications?

In this chapter we shall consider a pastor's qualifications along three lines: natural, educational, and spiritual, leaving the most important to the last.

I. NATURAL QUALIFICATIONS

By this term we refer to qualifications that belong to a man's human nature. They are no indications of spirituality, for many of them are possessed by unsaved people and by those who are not in the pastorate. But they should be present in every man who feels called to pastoral work. Some may have them to a greater degree than others, but they should at least be present in every pastor. The order in which we give them here is not always the order of importance.

It is very important for a pastor to have *mental and nervous stability*. He must be able to remain calm in the face of the most distressing circumstances. He will be called to sickbeds, scenes of accident, homes of bereavement, and to other places where people have gone all to pieces. His steadying and assuring voice may do a great deal to restore order and calm. It will often be his responsibility to be the bearer of sad news and he must find the best way of approach. A man died suddenly at a Sunday night union meeting held in the village park. His pastor went to the home immediately after the close of the service to see what help he could render. The man was in his fifties but had never been married. He lived together with his unmarried sister, a few years younger than he. She was nowhere around, for she had also been at the park but had been sitting in a car. She had noticed the commotion when she saw

23

a man being carried out but had no idea that it was her brother. The men who had brought the body home were still there. In just a few minutes the sister arrived from the meeting unaware of what had happened. Who do you suppose was delegated to bring her the shocking news?

Many similar, sometimes even worse, experiences will fall to a pastor's lot and he must be able to be quiet and calm even if everybody else is upset and excited.

It is just as important for a pastor to have a *sympathetic nature*. This will keep him from becoming hardened through frequent contact with difficulties and hard experiences. He must never allow himself to become professional and callous. On occasion he may have to be very firm and appear not to be sensitive enough, but this should never rob him of the ability to enter into the joys and sorrows of the people with whom he deals. For example, at funerals some morticians crack jokes and tell funny stories to the minister while in the office before the service begins. It will create a bad impression on the mourners if they walk past the open door and see the pastor laugh, or even smile. His message will not bring any comfort to them. Similarly, after the service some pastors have been indiscreet enough to behave in such a way as to appear to be without sympathy.

A teen-age boy hated his father and planned to poison him. He put some poison into the water bottle which was kept in the refrigerator. His sister, knowing nothing of his scheme, came into the house very thirsty and took a deep drink out of that bottle. In a few minutes she was dead. It was a very sad funeral conducted by the girl's pastor, assisted by the pastor of her parents. While the people stood on the porch after the service waiting for the corpse to be carried to the hearse, the man who had preached the sermon began to talk in a loud voice about his golf score that summer. It was a breach of good manners, besides failing to bring any comfort to the bereaved family.

God's Word says, "Rejoice with them that do rejoice, and weep with them that weep" (Romans 12:15). Sometimes it is easier to do the weeping than the rejoicing. Sometimes a pastor has to do both the same day. He may have a very sad funeral in the afternoon and a wedding at night.

The word "sympathy" is from the Greek and literally means *to suffer together with*. It means to enter into the sorrows of another as far as possible. It means to make another's sorrow his own. Sympathy should be shown to strangers as well as to members of the church. Occasionally the bodies of people who had moved from the community are shipped back for burial. The pastor of one of the local churches is called upon to conduct a brief service at the grave. The tendency will be to conduct it perfunctorily and in a purely professional way. Possibly the chief mourners will not be present. Perhaps the pastor did not know the departed, but even under such conditions he should conduct himself with dignity and not rush through the service without any feeling.

A pastor should be *interested in people*. If he stays long enough in one place, he should know the members of his church quite thoroughly. The better he knows them, the better he will understand them. It is not enough to stand in the church door and shake hands with men and women as they leave the service and say, "How do you do?" or, "How are you feeling?" That means no more than the average remark by the people who shake hands with the pastor after he has poured out his heart in a very earnest sermon and say, "I enjoyed your little talk very much," or, "That was a nice message," etc. It is merely an expression of politeness.

People will easily sense insincerity and professionalism in the pastor. How can he show a real interest in people? There are a number of things that could and should be done. Most people appreciate it if he remembers something about them, even if it is only their name at first. After that he should know some things about the family, especially the children and their names. He should know and remember the daily occupation of all his members, and any problem they may have. He should know what his young people are studying in high school and college and ask intelligent questions about their subjects. In other words, he should enter into all the experiences of his people, especially their joys and sorrows.

Being interested in people will help the pastor to understand them better. His social contacts must be carefully guarded, but there must never be a sign of aloofness to frighten people away. Through social contact the pastor will learn to know and understand his people. And understanding them will help him to plan the messages he is to preach to them.

The author's father was not a pastor nor a psychologist, nor even an educated man, but he always used to say to his children, "It is a great art to learn to get along with people." We believe he was right, and a pastor should *be able to get along with people* more than anyone else. It seems that some pastors never learn it and consequently have very short pastorates. We once met a man who had been the pastor of about 35 churches in 30 years. He was a good preacher, and it was not his preaching that was the reason for his short pastorates. Somehow it seems he always managed to offend some of his people in a short time, and so seriously that he was no longer wanted as pastor by that church.

To be able to get along with people is especially important in a man's first pastorate. He may be filled with great ideas of his importance. He may be determined to *run* the church, no matter how many members he loses, just so he is on top. That is the wrong attitude. There are times when members must be disciplined, or even removed from membership, but generally speaking a pastor should learn to get along with the people in his church. This does not require any compromise of his message. If the church is in a low spiritual state when he assumes the pastorate, he should pray and labor to lift it to a higher plane, always remembering that it is better to lead than to drive. As long as possible, gentle measures should be used to accomplish this end. If drastic steps are necessary, the pastor should not be afraid to take them, but it should be done in love. He should not become known as a "boss," or as one who always carries "a chip on his shoulder."

All this requires *tact*, and tact has been defined as "the ability to deal with others without giving offense." Some pastors seem to lack this quality. Their intentions may be good but they have a weakness for saying the right word at the wrong time, or saying the wrong word at the right time. Both are equally bad.

A pastor should have an *appreciation of responsibility*, a realization of the seriousness of his ministry. What he says and does may influence men for good or evil; through him men may be saved, but they may also be lost. He is a "marked man," especially in a small community. He must take himself seriously, yet not to the extent of making a fool of himself. He must be able to appreciate the humor of certain situations also.

A pastor is a man who must be *willing to work hard*. This is very important. If he entered the ministry because he thought it was easy, he will soon be disillusioned — that is, if he is a real pastor. He needs to work hard as a student in preparation for pastoral work. As a pastor, he needs to work hard in his study. He should not be satisfied with the knowledge of the Bible he gained in school but must keep on studying. His sermons will soon show it if he doesn't. And then he must be willing to work hard in his parish. In a small community he should make an earnest effort to know all the people. And he should know what is going on in the community.

A true pastor should also be possessed of a *spirit of hopefulness*. He must be realistic enough to face facts just as they are, yet optimistic enough to hope for the best no matter how discouraging the outlook may be. This applies to his person, his problems in the church, and the individual members with whom he has to deal.

II. EDUCATIONAL QUALIFICATIONS

How much education should a pastor have? That depends somewhat on his age at the time he obeyed the divine call. If he is a young man, he should get all the education he can. If he is not so young any more, he should still seek to advance educationally as far as it is possible. Furthermore, any pastor should remain a student all his life. Let us suggest briefly the courses of study to be pursued. (It is taken for granted that the ministerial candidate has been graduated from high school.)

1. *A good Bible course.* Such courses are offered in good Bible institutes or Bible colleges. The training given in these schools acquaints the student with the contents and the teachings of the whole Bible. In a good school he will be taught to see the Bible as a connected whole, not merely a collection of pious writings. If for any reason it becomes necessary to choose between a Bible course and a college course, the Bible course is the more important. A knowledge of college subjects is of great value; a thorough knowledge of the Bible is essential.

2. *A liberal arts education.* In our day many colleges put the emphasis on science. This seems to be especially true of the great state universities. This is an age of science and invention. Wonderful discoveries have been made and marvelous inventions produced. By many these are considered the most important things in the world. It is surprising how many preachers one can find who started out by taking a course in engineering. After they were saved and became obedient to the Lord's call, they changed their course. A liberal arts course is a much better foundation for theological studies than a course in science. In most good seminaries the student who wishes to be graduated with the bachelor of divinity degree (B.D.) must enter with a bachelor of arts (A.B.) degree from an accredited college. Such subjects as literature, languages, history, philosophy, and other liberal arts subjects will be a great help in further study. There is enough science in the liberal arts course to meet the needs of a pastor.

But let us take the time to point out that sometimes it has pleased the Lord to take a man with no formal education, such as D. L. Moody, and make of him the greatest evangelist of his era. He does it, we believe, to show that the real power of a preacher is the spiritual power. But few uneducated ministers have ever had a successful career. Some of the men greatly used of God in the Bible were highly educated men, e. g., Moses, Daniel, and Paul.

3. *A seminary course.* A theological seminary has as its one purpose the training of men for the ministry. It offers graduate courses in the Bible. It teaches the student how to analyze and interpret the Bible. Most seminaries give courses in Greek and Hebrew, the original languages of the Bible. There are courses in church history, acquainting the student with the development of Christianity from the time of Christ. There are courses in homiletics, giving instructions in the best methods of presenting the message. All has been planned for the man who is going to be a preacher.

A parallel can be drawn between the physical and spiritual worlds in the amount of training one has. In the physical realm we can recognize three levels of service: the one who is able to administer first aid, the practicing physician, and the specialist. In the event of an accident, the one who is able to render first aid is very valuable. But for further treatment and in the case of illness, you would call for a qualified physician. And then there are some cases that require the service of a specialist.

There *is* a place for an expert personal worker or lay evangelist. Sometimes such men also become excellent preachers. A better education as a rule serves as a better preparation for the more difficult work of pastoring a church. And there is a need for specialists in spiritual work. Such a man was the late professor of Princeton, Robert Dick Wilson. He spent fifteen years studying the languages of Biblical countries, fifteen years in doing research work in the literature available in these languages, and the remaining years of his life in giving the results to the world. His was the work of a specialist and has done much to corroborate the authenticity and integrity of the Old Testament. Such was also the service of Dr. Melvin Grove Kyle, of the Xenia-Pittsburgh Theological Seminary, who spent years in archaeological research in the Holy Land and did much to confirm our faith in the historicity of the Old Testament. Sir William Ramsey did the same kind of work for the New Testament, especially the writings of Luke in his gospel and the Acts.

The educational preparation of the ministerial candidate should be adequate for the work he expects to do.

III. SPIRITUAL QUALIFICATIONS

As a preparation for the ministry these are more important qualifications than talents, education, favorable circumstances, or the ability to preach. If a man fails here, all his other qualifications will not be able to make him a successful pastor.

The first spiritual qualification of a pastor is that he must be a Christian. The man who expects to dispense spiritual truth must have experienced that which he expects others to believe. Without the new birth he has no adequate conception of spiritual things, no clear understanding of Christian experience, no ability to lead others to faith in Jesus Christ, nor is he able to build up the church of Christ. One would hardly think that a man who has no saving faith in Christ would undertake pastoral work, and yet such is often the case.

In addition to being born again, the pastor should be a Spirit-filled man (Ephesians 5:18). We would like to say he *must* be Spirit-filled, but that would raise the standard so high that very few would qualify. At least he should constantly strive to be filled with the Spirit. The apostle Peter was Spirit-filled when he preached the great sermon on the Day of Pentecost and on many other occasions (Acts 2:4, 14; 4:8, 31, etc.), but not when he played the part of a hypocrite in Antioch of Syria (Galatians 2:11-13). There he allowed the flesh to dominate. The temptation to disobey the Spirit will ever be present. Every time a pastor yields to it, his ministry is weakened.

There are good reasons why the pastor should be filled with the Spirit of God. It is commanded by God and he needs it in order to understand the Word he is preaching. Bible analysis and exegesis will help him, but they are no substitute for the filling with the Spirit. The Word of God was given by inspiration of the Spirit of God, and the Spirit alone is capable of giving the proper interpretation (I Corinthians 2:14). A man may be highly educated and yet fail to grasp the spiritual message of the Bible.

Another reason is that the pastor might preach the Word with power. It was not Peter's personality, education, or persuasiveness that accomplished the great results on the Day of Pentecost, but the power of the Spirit who filled him. To have this power one must unreservedly yield himself to the control of the Holy Spirit.

The pastor should have some *experience* (some say success) *in Christian work* before he undertakes to lead a church. It is most unwise, generally speaking, to take a man who has been recently saved and done no Christian work of any kind, and make him the pastor of a church. Paul warns against the use of a novice in such a responsible position (I Timothy 3:6). He should at least have served in some capacity in the church, as a teacher in the Sunday school, a young people's leader, a personal worker. Every bit of work he has done for the Lord will be helpful to him after he becomes a pastor.

> Give of your best to the Master,
>   Naught else is worthy His love;
> He gave Himself for your ransom,
>   Gave up His glory above;
> Laid down His life without murmur,
>   You from sin's ruin to save,
> Give Him your heart's adoration,
>   Give Him the best that you have.
>   — H. G. Barnard

CHAPTER 4

THE PASTOR'S ORDINATION

Most churches are pastored by ordained ministers, that is, men who have been set apart for the ministry of the Gospel, usually by what is called an "ordination service." The definition of the word sometimes given is not of much help to Protestants, for it defines "ordination" as "the conferring of holy orders." The meaning is that it conveys the authority to perform all the functions of a pastor.

I. IS ORDINATION NECESSARY?

Is it necessary for a man to be ordained in order to preach the Gospel? The answer is an unqualified no. It is no more necessary to be ordained in order to preach than it is to be baptized in order to be saved.

Dwight L. Moody, the great American evangelist of the latter half of the nineteenth century, was never ordained. We have been told that when he inquired about becoming ordained he was told he did not have enough education. Yet Moody was a man of great spiritual power and was used in bringing many souls to Christ. When in London he preached in the Royal Albert Hall with members of the royal family in attendance.

Charles H. Spurgeon, famous pastor of the Metropolitan Tabernacle, London, never received ordination. He revolted against Anglican sacerdotalism "which seemed to hold that in the imposition of hands in ordination divine grace trickled down through a bishop's fingertips, and he felt moved to protest against it."[1]

A dearly beloved friend of the author came from the (Plymouth) Brethren. Eventually he formed an independent church and became its pastor, serving until the end of his days. He had been a preacher and a pastor for many years before he asked for ordination. But when he was convinced of its scripturalness he did not hesitate to submit himself to a council of men, who were all younger than he, for examination and ordination. It was the right spirit of humility which helps to adorn the doctrines of Christ.

[1]A. H. Strong, *Systematic Theology.*

31

Why then do Protestants believe in and practice ordination? What is ordination? One definition says that it means: "To invest with ministerial and sacerdotal functions; to introduce into the office of the Christian ministry." The first half does not express what is held by most Protestants, but we can agree with the second half.

We object to the claim that it "invests with sacerdotal functions." What is sacerdotalism? The dictionary answer: "The doctrine that ordination confers special powers and rights for the exercise of the ministry." To some this seems to mean that thereafter certain acts performed by the ordained man (such as baptism, the administration of the Lord's Supper) will have actual spiritual merit because of the man who performs them. Most Protestants, except the Anglicans, do not believe in this kind of sacerdotalism; but generally they do believe in a public service in which a man is set apart for definite Christian work. It qualifies him to perform all the functions of the ministerial office. We do not believe that ordination conveys any spiritual authority.

There are a few legal benefits that are extended by most of our state governments to an ordained man. One of these is the right to officiate at marriages. This is not true universally. To be a pastor is sufficient in most places. It is also necessary to be an ordained man to become a chaplain in the Armed Forces of the United States. However, there are also certain educational requirements that must be met in order to become a chaplain.

There are some services from which an ordained minister is exempt. He is not required to go into military service, nor is it necessary for him to serve on a jury.

II. Is THERE A SCRIPTURAL BASIS FOR ORDINATION?

We believe there is. There are a number of passages in which some form of the word "ordained" is used.

1. Jesus "ordained" the Twelve before He sent them out to preach (Mark 3:14). However, the word used is translated from the Greek which means "to make." This indicates that Jesus *made* these men His apostles by appointing them to this office.

2. Paul says he was "ordained a preacher" (I Timothy 2:7). The word used has a similar meaning — to put, set, or make. Paul seems to have in mind the thought that God put him into that office.

3. Paul and Barnabas on their missionary journey "ordained" elders in every church (Acts 14:23). The word used literally means

"to vote by stretching out the hand."[2] It would seem to indicate appointment by the uplifted hand.

4. Paul directed Titus to "ordain" elders (Titus 1:5). The Greek word also means to put, set, or appoint. In none of these places does it convey the idea of conferring authority.

But we can sum up a few thoughts from these verses. (1) The Lord *makes* His own servants and appoints them to their work. (2) Other preachers, no doubt with the consent and cooperation of the church, recognize God's call. (3) From this it seems evident that a candidate was examined for his fitness by those who ordained him.

It seems to have become the custom quite early in the Christian Church "to set apart" a man for the work of preaching and the performance of pastoral duties by the "laying on of hands" (see Acts 13:3; I Timothy 4:14; 5:22; II Timothy 1:6; also Acts 6:6 which refers to deacons). So we believe that ordination has a Scriptural basis and for this reason has been practiced in the Christian Church down through the centuries of the Christian era.

III. WHO IS TO BE ORDAINED?

Is the church expected to ordain anyone who desires ordination? The answer is an unqualified no. In many local congregations there appear individuals who are obsessed with the idea that they should preach, and of course they want to be ordained. It would be a serious mistake for a church to grant such requests. There are several criteria by which we can determine who is qualified for ordination.

The person to be ordained must be convinced that *God has called him to this ministry*. The apostle Paul said: "For though I preach the gospel, I have nothing to glory of; for necessity is laid upon me: yea, woe is unto me, if I preach not the gospel!" (I Corinthians 9:16). Let us remember that ordination in itself does not make any man a pastor or minister, nor does it endue him with special qualifications for the work. There must be first the absolute conviction that God has called him. There is danger of minimizing the call of God. This is doubtless the reason why there are men in the pulpit whom God has not called. They give proof of this by the message they preach. It stands to reason that God would not call a man to preach contrary to the Bible. The lack of this conviction is doubtless the reason why many men forsake the ministry. The work is more difficult than they expected and the

2Thayer's *Greek Lexicon.*

income is below what they desired, so they leave the pastorate and find secular employment that pays better wages.

The person to be ordained must *give evidence of having been called of God.* There are several ways in which this can be done.

(1) By the expression of his own conviction (I Corinthians 9:16; I Timothy 1:12). That is why at an examination for ordination the candidate is asked to give an account of his call to the ministry. This is where modern councils sometimes fail. If the candidate is well educated, little attention is paid to his call or even his doctrinal position.

(2) By his ability to preach. In describing the qualifications of a bishop (pastor), Paul says that he must be "apt to teach" (I Timothy 3:2). To Timothy he gives the command to "preach the word" (II Timothy 4:2). There is a difference between teaching and preaching. Those who are called to the ministry should be both "pastors and teachers" (Ephesians 4:11). Teaching means "to impart knowledge." The aim of teaching is that the student should have more knowledge when he leaves a class than when he entered it. We are not now concerned with the method of teaching, only with the aim and the results. Preaching means "to proclaim the gospel message; to deliver a sermon, to exhort." The aim of preaching is to produce action. The word translated "preach" comes from a Greek word (Galatians 5:11) which means that something ought to be done. There are some pastors who are excellent Bible teachers but they do not produce many converts. There are other preachers who are always evangelistic and have many converts, but their members never become strong Christians because they have no Bible teaching. The ideal for a pastor is to have a combination of both.

Why did Paul choose Timothy as an associate in the gospel ministry? Doubtless God directed him, but it was also because Timothy had a good reputation in the local church (Acts 16:1-3). The brethren spoke well of him. No doubt this refers to all of his life. He conducted himself as was becoming to a Christian young man. We believe it also implies that Timothy had shown some ability as a preacher. Was Timothy ever ordained? Without any doubt, for what else could Paul mean by "the laying on of hands by the presbytery" (I Timothy 4:14)? But does Paul mean that the gift of preaching was given to Timothy *through* the laying on of hands? If so, is it true in every ordination? No; the fact that Timothy had a good reputation *before* Paul chose him bears this out. The preposition *meta* (translated "with," I Timothy 4:14) sometimes means only accompaniment, not instrumentality. Timothy already had natural gifts; at the time of his ordination, a special spiritual gift was imparted to him. We believe this should be an accompaniment of every Scriptural ordination, but it is often missing.

By whom was Timothy ordained? In the Authorized Version they are called "presbyters"; some other versions translate the word and call them "elders." It does not say whether they all came from one church or more. If from only one church, it would be an argument for a plurality of elders in a single congregation. If from more than one, it is an argument for an ordination council made up of representatives from several churches.

There is another point to be considered as to who should be ordained or how the qualifications for ordination are to be determined, and that is by the conviction of the church. We believe this is the meaning of I Timothy 3:2-7. Who would know whether a candidate for ordination measures up to this high standard or not except the local church of which he is a member? Unless the church is convinced that the man is called of God by his having given proof of his ministry, it should not call an ordination council.

IV. WHO DECIDES WHOM TO ORDAIN?

This question grows out of what we have just discussed. The gist of Dr. C. I. Scofield's remarks on Titus 1:5 are helpful here. He points out that while elders are "set" in the churches by the Holy Spirit, great stress is laid upon their due appointment (Acts 14:23; Titus 1:5). At first they were ordained (Greek *cheirotoneo,* "to elect," "to designate with the hand") by an apostle (Acts 14:23); but in Titus and I Timothy the qualifications of an elder became a part of the Scriptures for the guidance of the churches in such appointment (I Timothy 3:1-7; see *Scofield Reference Bible,* comment on Titus 1:5).

Titus was directed to "ordain elders in every city." It seems that there were qualified men in these churches; the question is altogether one of appointment. We infer from this that the decision to ordain these men was not vested in Titus; he was to see to it that it was done.

In several places we read of "elders" laying on the hands (Acts 13:3; I Timothy 4:14). However, in the first passage only the pronoun "they" is used. Some take this to refer to the whole church, and perhaps correctly so.

We can only draw inferences from these statements, and we have concluded that it is within the authority of the local church to vote to "set apart" a man called of God to pastoral work. **Can** a local church ordain a man without consulting anyone else? This is being done by the great Moody Memorial Church of Chicago, and we believe it is Scriptural. A local church may overrule the adverse recommendation of a council and proceed to ordain a candidate in spite of the decision of the council.

V. IS AN EXAMINATION NECESSARY BEFORE ORDINATION?

None is definitely prescribed in the New Testament. However, in giving instructions to Titus regarding the qualifications of a "bishop" (or "elder"), Paul says he should be a man "holding fast the faithful word as he hath been taught, that he may be able by sound doctrine both to exhort and to convince the gainsayer" (Titus 1:9). How can this be discovered except by an examination? In the past some churches (Mennonites, for example) elected men and authorized them to preach without ordaining them. If their conduct and their talents, plus their adherence to the fundamental doctrines of the Bible, seemed to qualify them, an ordination was arranged for without a special examination. But even where there is an examination, a candidate may be able to conceal his true convictions. On one occasion a young man was being examined who was said to hold certain liberal views. When questioned on some points, he always prefaced his answer by saying: "Dr. Strong (referring to A. H. Strong's *Systematic Theology*) says so and so." The answers were perfectly orthodox. The council passed him. Afterwards the candidate boasted to one of his friends that he had not committed himself at all; he had only answered what Dr. Strong said.

Are the candidates examined always approved for ordination? Not necessarily. The author has sat on councils where the candidate was very indefinite on some of the fundamental doctrines, and the council's adverse recommendation was accepted by the church. Let it be noted that this is the exception rather than the rule.

Should a man be ordained unless he has a call to a church? We doubt if this is advisable in the usual cases. There might be exceptions to this rule. According to the New Testament pattern, there were always churches before there were elders. With the number of graduates streaming from seminaries, Bible colleges, and Bible institutes every year, there would be the danger of having more ordained ministers than there were churches, in denominational and also in independent churches. Besides, having been called to a church may be an indication that the call of the Lord rests upon the man.

Can only ordained men ordain others? It seems clear that men not ordained to the ministry can administer baptism (Acts 8:38), and if so they can surely also ordain. Unless we take this position, we will soon have what the Roman church has — sacerdotalism. We believe that by implication the Scriptures sanction the calling of an ordination council which examines the candidate and then brings its recommendation to the church.

VI. SHOULD A MAN BE LICENSED BEFORE HE IS ORDAINED?

There is no Scriptural precedent nor any teaching on the subject. Some churches have practiced it in the past, and some still do. While we do not argue in favor of it, we believe it has its good points: (1) It will show if a man has any talent for preaching and pastoral work; (2) it will reveal how much knowledge he has of the Word of God; (3) it will disclose his doctrinal position; (4) it will be especially beneficial if it gives him some practical experience in pastoral work. We are of the opinion that an "internship" in pastoral services might be of great benefit. A doctor of medicine, although he has been graduated from his course in medicine, is not licensed until he has served an internship of two years in the state in which he wishes to practice. Why should not theological graduates have similar training before becoming pastors and being ordained to the ministry?

VII. CALLING AN ORDINATION COUNCIL

Before concluding this chapter, we want to say a word about the procedure in calling for an ordination council, and also the usual procedure of an ordination service. This applies to churches with a congregational form of government.

When a church which has been served by an unordained man comes to the conclusion that the pastor is qualified for ordination, it declares this conviction by a congregational vote. A date is set for the examination of the candidate and a number of churches are invited to send their pastor and two other members to help form a council. Some denominations have rigid rules in this matter and in some places there is a "Permanent Council" appointed for this purpose by the denomination. Our suggestions relate to the old Baptist and Congregational order and to the custom followed by many churches today. Usually it is planned to have the examination in the afternoon and the ordination in the evening of the same day. More recently ordinations have been conducted a few days after the examination. This causes less embarrassment if there is an adverse recommendation. The inviting church usually furnishes a free meal to the council, especially if the examination and the ordination occur on the same day.

At the meeting of the council, the church clerk reads the minutes of the church at which action relative to the ordination was taken. Then he presides at the election of a moderator (temporary or permanent). The elected moderator conducts the election of a clerk. A list of all the churches represented and their delegates is then made up. This constitutes the council. Then it is time for the actual examination to begin. Sometimes there is prayer at the very beginning, sometimes just before the examination.

The council examines the candidate on three points: (1) his Christian experience; (2) his call to the ministry; (3) his doctrinal position. The council determines whether to hear the whole statement at once or to allow questions in between. Sometimes the questioning is delayed until the candidate has fully expressed himself. It is unfortunate that in some instances members of the council ask questions which pertain to a pet theory of their own and on which there are many different opinions. The questions should relate definitely to the candidate's position on fundamental doctrines and his qualifications as a minister of the Word of God.

After the examination, the candidate is dismissed and the council goes into private session. It decides on whether or not to recommend to the church to proceed as planned. It sometimes happens that the decision is in the negative. The church can then decide whether or not to abide by the council's recommendation. The candidate is then notified of the council's decision. If it is favorable, a committee is appointed to arrange the program for the ordination service. This may consist of the candidate, the moderator or clerk, and the candidate's pastor, if he is present. There is no hard and fast rule about this.

We give just a brief outline of the program usually followed at an ordination service.

Prayer by the moderator.
Congregational singing
Reading of the council's recommendation
Charge to the candidate
Charge to the church
Ordination sermon
Laying on of hands by all ordained ministers present
Ordination prayer by someone previously appointed
Extending the hand of fellowship
Benediction

The program may be varied to suit local conditions.

CHAPTER 5

THE PASTOR'S SPIRITUAL LIFE

President Woodrow Wilson, speaking to a group of ministers and other Christian workers, stated that his father, who was a Presbyterian minister, used to say: "The Christian minister must *be* something before he can *do* anything." He did not mean that he must have accomplished something that seemed great to himself and others, but he referred to the character which the Christian worker must have.

We consider the pastor's spiritual life first because that is the most important. The character of the lawyer does not affect the quality of his professional service very much. The manufacturer or merchant may at heart be a scoundrel without hurting his business. There are doctors whose character is open to question but who are still good in their profession. In our day there are even teachers whose moral standards are not very high who are yet considered to be good teachers. But this can never be true of a minister of the Gospel. The value of his work is measured by the conviction that he lives what he preaches. If he fails to do so, his work is of little value.

In giving the charge to a young minister at his ordination, an old Scotch minister, said:

> The great purpose for which a minister is settled in a parish is not to cultivate scholarship, or to visit the people during the week, or even to preach to them on Sunday; but it is to live among them as a good man, whose mere presence is a demonstration that cannot be gainsaid, that there is a life possible on earth which is fed from no earthly source, and that the things spoken of on Sunday in the church are realities.[1]

It is impossible to make a sharp distinction between the spiritual and the secular because the spiritual life enters into everything else. This should be true of all Christians, but especially so in the career of a pastor.

Regardless of whether we believe in dichotomy or trichotomy, all of us are convinced that man has a physical life and a spiritual

[1]A. S. Hoyt, *The Preacher* (New York: Hodder and Stoughton, 1909), p. 159.

life. In the plan of God, the spiritual was intended to predominate. The human spirit indwelt by the Holy Spirit is to control the body, and not vice versa. The needs, appetites, and desires of the body and the mind should not have control over any man's life, much less that of a pastor.

I. THE MEANING OF THE SPIRITUAL LIFE

Let us consider the subject negatively and positively.

What It Does Not Mean

There are a few things which are falsely considered to be a part or indicative of the pastor's spiritual life.

1. *A sanctimonious appearance.* That idea of a Christian minister is commonly presented in cartoons — a tall, thin man wearing a long black coat, having a huge hooked nose and a pair of *pince nez* glasses clipped to it, with a very somber look on his face — to the extent that people have begun to think of him as such. But a Roman Catholic priest is usually presented as a very kind, understanding, fatherly sort of man, who is unselfishly helpful to all in a community. Of course the picture is not a true one.

2. *Distinct clothing.* The author comes from a Mennonite background, and not a great many years ago the Mennonites believed that a true Christian had to wear plain clothes and no jewelry at all. If he did so, he "conformed to the world." In dress and in all matters, the pastor was expected to set the right example. In our day such radical departures from prevailing styles make the individual much more conspicuous than if he dresses so as not to call attention to himself. The pastor should not be conspicuous for either the plainness of his garb or its extravagance.

What about wearing a clerical garb? There are arguments on both sides of the question. Against it is the idea that it makes too much difference between the clergy and the laity. In favor of it is the fact that it makes a minister easily recognizable. Some good Protestant ministers always dress like clergymen when they travel. It often gives them opportunities for service which might not come to them otherwise. At formal services, such as a church wedding, we believe it is advisable to be in formal dress for the occasion.

What about wearing a pulpit robe? There have been arguments that this makes a service too formal but in general the attitude has changed. In even small churches the choirs are often robed, and so why should not the pastor? But in many small churches this would seem out of order. This is a matter of individual taste, and also the custom of the community or denomination.

In his week-day activities, even when he goes calling, the pastor should wear clothes like other people. In a small town everyone knows who the minister is, regardless of how he is dressed. In the city it might be helpful to wear distinctive garb when he is calling on strangers on behalf of the church.

The principal thing we wish to emphasize here is that the spiritual life does not depend on the clothes he wears.

3. *Pious words and phrases.* There are ministers who think it makes them sound very pious and spiritual if they are able to make some pious remark on every occasion. Some have exaggerated opinions of the impression they make on others. There are times when it is proper to administer reproof, but even this can be done in a way that does not impress the hearers as an attempt to show off superior spirituality.

A pastor was fishing from a dock along with a number of other men. He introduced himself as the pastor of a small church in a neighboring town. One of the men remarked facetiously, "Well, I am glad you told us; I am going to watch my language while you are here." Evidently he thought his words would create a laugh at the preacher's expense. To his surprise the minister replied with a smile, "Well, I suppose I could stand a little of it; the Lord has to hear it all the time." That was a rebuke with a punch, and the one who administered it rose in the esteem of those that heard it.

4. *Ascetical practices.* The members of certain Roman Catholic orders are required to practice asceticism. It means the devotion to a contemplative life, a life which through self-torture or self-denial can be disciplined to a high spiritual or intellectual state.

Some of this spirit was present in Puritanism. The Puritans did not believe in showing joy in anything physical. Nor did they deem it proper to display sorrow. There may be a few who hold such views today, but their number is not large. No one will be attracted to the Christian life by such conduct. A sense of humor is very helpful in a Christian worker, and "a merry heart doeth good like medicine" (Proverbs 17:22).

Dr. H. A. Ironside has called attention to the fact that it says in the Bible, "Enoch walked with God... and begat sons and daughters" (Genesis 5:22). He deduces from this that there is nothing in the normal family life that militates against fellowship with God.[2]

5. *A spirit of mysticism.* We agree that the mystics of past

[2]H. A. Ironside, *The Continual Burnt Offering* (New York: Loizeaux Brothers, 1943), meditation for January 3.

years had some very wrong conceptions—at least some of them did. But they also had some things that were very good. They were wrong in believing that they could speak with the authority of inspiration because of the intimacy of their association with God. They were right in believing that every Christian should have personal communion with God. We mention this to warn against the extreme views held and advanced by some.

What Is Meant by Spiritual Life

There is such a thing as Scriptural pietism, which holds to the reality of the spiritual life. Spener and Francke, leaders in the missionary movement after the Reformation, were pietists. It was a reaction against the dead orthodoxy of that period. There is such a thing as dead orthodoxy in our day. That is what the Pharisees had. They were very careful about observing even the minutest detail of the Law, and yet their walk was far from a spiritual walk. There are people like them in our churches today. They hold correct doctrine and are very critical of those who hold other views, but they have very little, if any, spiritual life themselves. The spiritual life is just as real as the physical life. Every pastor should know and realize that in his own experience.

1. *Mental and spiritual unselfishness.* Let us illustrate what we mean. Do you prepare your sermon in a noisy room where all kinds of other things are going on at the same time — where the children are quarreling as they play; where the radio is on and someone is making a speech, or a jazzy commercial is being sung; where your wife is busy with the sewing machine or the vacuum sweeper? Or do you seek the quiet privacy of your study? Most men prefer quietness and no interruption. But if you are in your study and pursuing some rich but somewhat elusive line of thinking, and the phone rings, or someone comes to see you with a very simple problem — it may be someone whose story you have heard before and know what is coming — can you leave your work and in a sweet spirit deal with your caller? What is more, can you go back after the caller has gone and pick up the threads of your thought as though nothing had happened? It is not easy for some men, and for such it might be wiser not to have a telephone in the study.

There are some men who do not permit anything except an emergency to interrupt them when they are studying. But we are of the opinion that a Christian minister is obligated to interrupt whatever he is doing and see what help he can render to whosoever calls on him. That is what we mean by mental and spiritual un-selfishness.

2. *A spirit of humility.* Humility is an almost unknown quality of Christian character today. A great many people in our churches do not want a humble man as their pastor. They want a "big shot," even in some of the small churches. If the pastor does not boast about himself, they think "he hasn't got what it takes." The apostle Paul resorted to boasting only when his apostleship had been called in question, and then he apologized profusely for it (II Corinthians 10-12).

A word of caution is in order here. For a pastor to be humble does not mean that he should let people walk all over him. If necessity requires, he should be willing to do anything, but ordinarily he has plenty of his own work to do which none of his members could perform. He did not accept the call to the church in order to become a messenger boy, or to serve as chauffeur for the ladies who want to go shopping at the county seat!

Let no man "think of himself more highly than he ought to think" (Roman 12:3). That applies to the pastor as well as to the members. It is nice to have people tell you they enjoyed your sermon, but quite frequently this is just a polite remark. Still there are some who devour every polite compliment and become greatly puffed up as a result. Some even begin to think they could handle much better and bigger churches, until they try it. Even then some did not profit by their experience, but found fault with the people who did not know how great a man their pastor was.

We are reminded of a man who preached an excellent sermon one Sunday. When he stood at the door afterward shaking hands with the worshipers, someone used very flattering words in praising that sermon — "It was a sermon that can't be beat." The preacher replied, "That's what the devil told me before I left the pulpit." We believe he did not mean to be rude, but he had to do something drastic to shake off the temptation to pride.

3. *Cheerfulness and gravity.* The two should go together because they will help the pastor to maintain a proper balance.

Cheerfulness comes first. There are many depressing experiences in a pastor's work. He has serious things to do and to think about, and he is in danger of talking more about trials than about God's mercies. Unless he knows how to maintain a cheerful spirit, he will soon become discouraged and give up the work. Cheerfulness has a reflexive value, but it is also contagious. Sometimes in a tense business meeting the injection of a bit of appropriate humor will bring a different spirit to the meeting. And cheerfulness is an indispensable quality when making sick calls.

But gravity is also important. There are men who think that to be a successful pastor one must know and be able to tell a lot of funny stories, crack all kinds of jokes, and turn every opportunity of life to wit. Some even tell risque stories and jokes, which are always out of order. There is a place for humor, but the man who carries the burden of the spiritual welfare of a community is not the proper man to act the clown or make himself the life of every party. Most people will appreciate a man who is balanced in these matters.

4. *Patience.* Patience is a very important part of spiritual life. There will come many times when you would like to see things go much faster, but you must remember that you cannot hurry the growing of a seed. Impatience is a sign of weakness. We have been told that on some mission fields the missionary who loses his temper in the presence of people of the land thereby loses all his influence. He might as well go home. The impatient pastor likewise loses much influence, with his own people and the people of the community.

5. *Spiritual Sensitivity.* It is very easy to become professional in all of our work for the Lord. Correct doctrine is important, but does not guarantee spirituality. There are preachers whose message is perfectly orthodox who are yet ugly, mean, selfish, self-assertive, and everything else but spiritual. It is possible to become hard and callous in defending the faith. It is one thing to "contend for the faith" (Jude vs. 3), but an altogether different matter to be "contentious" about the faith.

II. THE CULTIVATION OF THE SPIRITUAL LIFE

How shall these qualities be brought about and maintained? It is certain that they come from something deeper than formal orthodoxy, churchly attachment, and ordination to the ministry. A man may be an expert theologian and serve as the ordained minister of a church without being at all spiritually minded. He performs his services as any professional man would proceed. It behooves us to raise the question: What can a pastor do to develop these spiritual qualities? We make a few suggestions:

1. *Devotional reading of the Bible.* There will be a tendency after you become a pastor to read everything in the Bible with the idea of using it in a sermon some time. It is perfectly proper to be always on the lookout for sermonic material, but it is a serious mistake to neglect the reading of the Bible for personal

profit. The dietitian plans and supervises the preparation of meals for others, but she does not forget to partake of food herself.

Make it a habit to read something every day just for your own soul. Don't analyze every passage into so many homiletical points, or think of how you can use it to hit someone in your audience with it when you preach. Get all the good from it for your own self that you possibly can. It will acquaint you better with the Bible. It *will* help you in your preaching, but its first benefit should always be for your own soul.

2. *Daily and regular prayer.* It should not be necessary to say that a pastor ought to offer up thanks before eating a meal, yet we have seen pastors who failed to do so when eating in a public place, or even in a private dining room of a hotel.

It used to be that family worship was maintained in nearly every Christian home. In some places it was held mornings and evenings. There were some who read from the Bible before every meal. Now there are many pastors who have no family altar. In the modern city it is sometimes difficult to find a time that suits every member of the family, when some go to school and others go to work at different hours. But in a pastor's home there should always be time for it, and it should not be neglected.

But it is not enough for the pastor to have grace at table, or to have the family altar; he needs to take time for secret prayer. There are always many things about which he will want to confer with God, and it may be that it will consume much time every day. It is said that Martin Luther used to get up early in the morning in order to have enough time for prayer. Let us emphasize that this is *secret prayer.* It is altogether different from the pastoral prayer in the pulpit. Many things can be brought before the Lord in the secret prayer that it would be unwise to mention in public prayer, things about himself, his family, and members of his church.

A Pittsburgh pastor conducted a wonderful prayer campaign in his church one year. He took some six or seven names from the membership list in alphabetical order, and then selected the day and the hour when he would pray for them. He had approximately the same number each day. Then he wrote letters to those members giving them the day and the hour selected and suggested that they might join him in prayer at their home or in their office at the same time. It revived the life of the whole church.

It is very easy to become neglectful in the prayer life, as every man of experience will testify; but likewise every minister will confess that the most blessed times of his ministry were those when he was regular in prayer. And sometimes they were also the most difficult. You may not be able to become a "Praying Hyde," but a large place in your ministry should be given to prayer.

3. *Reading and meditation.* Of course a pastor should read his Bible, but also read other good books. They need not all be theological books or books on Bible study, though most of them should be in line with his calling. More will be said about this in the next chapter.

Having read, we need time to think about what we have read if it is to benefit us. When a pastor sits in his study staring out the window, or at some spot on the wall, he is not idle (or should not be). He should be meditating on something, perhaps on what he has just read. We wish we knew the author of the following quotation and could give credit for it. "There is no substitute for meditation. It is the most invigorating of heart tonics. And the stimulation is not quickly spent."

4. *Filled with the Spirit.* To be "filled with the Spirit" is a high ideal, but not unattainable. It means that every Christian worker should be constantly yielded to God so the Spirit can have His way in his life. Let no one say that he has attained, but let him constantly seek to be more Christ-like. The teaching is to all Christians: "Be filled with the Spirit" (Ephesians 5:18), but the pastor is expected to set the example.

5. *Conscientiousness.* There may arise occasions when the attention of the entire community is focused upon the pastor for some outstanding feat he has performed, but usually his daily life will not be spectacular. There is nothing sensational about looking after his family, correcting his children when they are disobedient, calling on some sick person, helping some student in high school with his Latin or geometry (if he is capable of doing so), assisting his wife with some task in the home, helping some member with a common chore, but it is all part of the spiritual life. Not only the man who prays much but also the one who serves much, is emphasizing the spiritual life.

6. *A pure life.* The pastor's spiritual life requires that he should lead a pure life: pure in acts, pure in speech, and pure even in his thoughts.

Of course, everyone knows that, but how many live up to it? The newspapers always use big headlines to publish the fact whenever a gospel minister has become involved in a moral scandal. And there are women who like nothing better than to become involved with the pastor in an illicit love affair. It is not necessary to make any further remarks here. Every pastor ought to know that it will ruin his ministry if it ever becomes known that he committed an act of immorality. Very capable men have had their ministry cut short on this account.

The world around us is constantly emphasizing sex and is doing its best to lower our moral resistance, but God's command to us is: "Watch ye, stand fast in the faith, quit you like men, be strong" (I Corinthians 16:13), and "having done all, to stand" (Ephesians 6:13).

"Take heed to the ministry which thou hast received in the Lord, that thou fulfill it" (I Corinthians 4:17).

CHAPTER 6

THE PASTOR'S INTELLECTUAL LIFE

Even if a pastor is the graduate of a Bible institute or of college and seminary, he should never think that his studying days are over when he receives his last diploma. The successful doctor of medicine is not satisfied when he has earned his degree and obtained his license to practice medicine. He will find ways and means to keep abreast of what is happening in the medical world. For example, in previous generations most drugs were derived from herbs, roots, flowers, etc. More recently, the medical profession has begun to rely almost entirely on chemicals, and these in general seem to be more effective. The herb doctor who did not keep up with developments was soon left far behind. Too often the pastor thinks his studying days are over when he comes out of school. But if a doctor finds constant further study and training necessary, so should the pastor.

Education cannot take the place of spirituality, but there is nevertheless a close connection between study and the spiritual life. The pastor who does not study will be found lacking in fresh spiritual experiences. We do not mean experiences not warranted by the Word of God, but those fresh glimpses of truth which come from the study of God's great revelation of Himself. The pastor who does not study will soon become stale in his preaching. He will be in danger of saying the same things in the same way over and over again until they become tiresome to his congregation. Sometimes it does not take long to reach this result.

Let it be remembered that the spiritual life comes first. A man may be a brilliant scholar but without spiritual power, while another man may lack some of the cultural polish given by education but successful in the ministry because of his reliance on God. But no Christian worker should cease studying after he has become settled in a pastorate or other place of Christian service.

The Scriptures endorse the view we are taking. Paul's advice to Timothy is familiar to all. "Study to shew thyself approved unto

God, a workman that needeth not to be ashamed, rightly dividing the word of truth" (II Timothy 2:15). The word "study" has been rendered "give diligence" (A S V), but study is one form of diligence.

Not quite so well known but equally important is another bit of advice from Paul to Timothy: "Meditate upon these things; give thyself wholly to them; that thy profiting may appear to all" (I Timothy 4:15). The verse that follows shows wherein he should meditate, and to what he should give himself wholly: "Take heed unto thyself, and unto the doctrine." He should give thought to his life and to his teaching.

And the apostle Peter, who did not have the formal education of the apostle Paul, said; "And beside this, giving all diligence, add to your faith virtue; and to virtue knowledge; and to knowledge temperance; and to temperance patience, and to patience godliness" (II Peter 1:5, 6). The addition of knowledge should not be omitted.

I. REASON FOR STUDYING

To what has already been said, we add several specific reasons why a pastor should continue to study.

1. *Because there is power in knowledge.* An old proverb says "Knowledge is power," and that is as true in preaching and pastoral work as anywhere else. Usually it is not very difficult to detect when a man's information is confined by the immediate limits of his subject. This is true about his preaching and also about his conversation. If he uses illustrations from science, he should know what he is talking about. A lack here will result in the lack of confidence in him on the part of those who are better informed.

2. *Because it will increase the respect of your people.* Even the small churches which we have in mind in this book are quite certain to have some young people who are going to college, or have college graduates in their membership. If what such people hear and see in their pastor leads them to believe that he is intellectually below their level, they will soon find his preaching tedious and boring. If they are true Christians, they may be polite enough to continue to come to the services, but his sermons will not touch them any more. If they are not real Christians, they may conclude, as many have done, that Christianity deals with a lot of generalities which are too superficial for them. It is often helpful when calling in homes where there are college students to ask intelligent questions about some of their courses in school. A young fellow once told me how his respect for his country pas-

tor greatly increased when he discovered that that man knew something about Latin and algebra.

3. *Because it will aid in sermon preparation.* Men candidating for a pulpit sometimes have only a limited number of good sermons. Naturally they will use their very best when they appear as candidates. Shortly after they are settled, their sermons become hum-drum and monotonous. Have you ever considered how many times a pastor has to preach in a year? There are 52 Sundays, and preaching twice on Sunday gives a total of 104 sermons. Even if you take out a few Sundays for vacation the total will still be around the hundred mark. Most likely he will bring a message at the mid-week service and this will add 52, or at least about 50, to the previous total. The man who stays in the same church as long as four years will have to face substantially the same audience approximately 600 times during that period. The experienced pastor can usually fall back on previously used messages, but it is different with the young fellow just out of school and in his first pastorate. Generally he will need a new sermon for each service. Unless he is a constant student, he will not be able to deliver sermons of a caliber suited to the needs of his people.

II. The Method of Studying

Quite naturally most of the pastor's studying will be conditioned by the nature of the work in which he is engaged. He will want to know the Bible better; he will want to understand the doctrinal position of the church he is serving; he will want to know all he can about the kind of people to whom he is ministering; he will want to be intelligent about current events.

1. *The private study of the Bible.* In school, you studied assigned portions every day. It will be different now that you are on your own. If there is a tendency to laziness in you, as there is in most of us, you will be in danger of relaxing and not studying more than just for each immediate service. This is sure to result in superficiality. In school you have had the general view of the Bible and its doctrines. You will have learned how to make an exegesis of certain portions of the Bible. The time has now come to make use of your training. The Bible should be the most prominent book in your study. Read it for devotional purposes; read it through as often as you can; read a portion of it studiously, if possible, every day. You will never know your Bible too well, or even well enough. Study for the sermons you are going to preach, but also study beyond your sermons. It will give you strong and

positive convictions. It is the chief instrument with which you will work.

2. *The use of other books.* If the pastor has not completed college or seminary, he should engage in the private study of at least the following subjects.

English. A pastor should know how to use correct English. It is surprising how many high school graduates today have practically no knowledge of correct English. People talk about having the gift of speaking in other tongues, but we have never yet met with one who received the gift of the English language without hard work. If a man uses slang or incorrect English, it should be made clear that he is doing it deliberately to emphasize a point, and not because of ignorance.

Theology. Theology is in reality a systematic study of all Christian doctrine. It is of importance next to the Bible itself. The pastor may never use theological expressions or formulae in his discourses, but the study will be a great help to him in getting a firm grasp of the whole subject of Christian doctrine.

The Bible, English and theology we put first, and in that order. The rest have not been arranged in any particular order. All are important and should be studied by all means.

Original Languages. Good translations of the Bible are available today, and the pastor should have a number of versions in his study. But it is still a good idea to be able to read from the original text.

Psychology. Psychology gives an insight into human nature and is especially valuable in pastoral counseling. Together with the Bible and much prayer, it will be very helpful in dealing with many of the problems encountered in pastoral work.

Sociology. This acquaints the student with the problems of society. Poverty, old age, race, slums, civic and community problems are all vital matters and belong to the realm of sociology.

Economics. Economics is the science that investigates the conditions and laws governing the production, distribution, and consumption of wealth, or the material means of satisfying human desires. We have a first hand acquaintance with the problems of economics, but we also need to get the angle of the other fellow.

Logic. Logic deals with orderly, critical thinking. It is always interesting to analyze the various campaign speeches in the year of a presidential election. All of them leave out some of the essentials — that is why one group is swayed by one man's arguments, and the other by his opponent's. Many sermons are based on very poor logic. They may move an illiterate, but seldom a thinking individual.

Archaeology. Archaeology provides much corroborative evidence for the veracity of the Bible. It is often useful as a means of enforcing an argument in a sermon. It may help to strengthen your own faith.

Natural Science. It is not enough for a preacher to get up and denounce the evolutionary theory and hold it up to ridicule; he ought to know what the theory really is, and what natural science is, so that he can discuss these subjects intelligently.

Missions. If the pastor knows little about missions, his church will know less. And the less a church does for missions the less life and power it will have.

These remarks by no means exhaust the subject, but we must stop here. They should help us to see that the best intellectual training a man can have is none too good for the work of the ministry.

Other Books. Have a book always handy, and be reading it. Someone has warned the pastor not to put "glass between himself and his books." This need not be taken literally, but the principle is good. Bishop Quayle's advice to young preachers was "Read many books." It is good advice. The Bible should come first, but along with it many other books.

Be careful not to read books on the same general subject all the time. It is one way of becoming lopsided in your preaching. There are pastors who delve so constantly in theology and philosophy that it is difficult for them to enter into a conversation about any other subjects.

Perhaps most of those who will read these lines will be of the conservative position in theology. To them we give the advice not to read so-called "fundamentalist" books only. We do not advocate a liberal theology, but we feel too often we are in danger of denouncing things without fully understanding them. Then, too, it will often strengthen our faith to read the other fellow's viewpoint. A man of the liberal school asked Dr. W. B. Riley if he would be willing to read at least one book on the liberal side of theology. He was surprised to learn that Dr. Riley had more books of that type in his library than he had of fundamentalist books. He was not a fundamentalist because of ignorance, as the so-called "modernists" usually think. My brother (Dr. H. C. Thiessen of Wheaton College) used to say, "Just because we are fundamentalists is no reason why we should not think."

Since these words are addressed to students on the various

sides of the millennial question, we think it in order to suggest that you should not read books on your side of the question only. If you are premillennial, make a point of reading postmillennial and amillennial writings. These writers have sound Bible teaching on other Bible subjects. Besides, the reading of the opposite viewpoint will not endanger your own position if your faith is based on conviction. Reading such books will enable you to speak with greater clearness when you present and defend your own.

Although your work is in the field of theology, do not read merely theological treatises, books of sermons, religious essays, etc. It will broaden your mind and develop you intellectually and culturally to read some other books too.

The pastor should read some current literature, including fiction. This does not include every "best-seller." He would not have time to read anything else if he did; besides, much of the modern fiction is so surrealistic that it would be a waste of time to read it. It is not necessary to finish the reading of a book of that kind if by some accident you have started it. Often it is enough to read a review of the new books in some secular magazine.

Someone has invented a good illustration explaining the difference between idealism, realism, and surrealism. An artist is in the country and decides to paint a picture of a farmer's large barn. It so happens that there is a manure pile in front of the barn, but the idealist omits that completely. He presents the barn as it ought to be, not as it is. The realist paints all that he sees, for he wants to portray the barn exactly as it is. Then along comes the surrealist and he paints the manure pile so large that you can hardly see the barn. He exaggerates what he sees because his mind is filled with such thoughts.

It is a good thing to read poetry. It is amazing to discover that there are preachers who have difficulty in scanning a poem and determining its meter. One pastor we knew used to talk about the "dumb poetry" he had read in a certain English course in college. He had never seen the beauty of a well-written poem. To him poems of Tennyson, Browning, and others, were on the same level as the Mother Goose rhymes! A pastor should have enough education to be able to distinguish between poetry and mere jingles. It is surprising to find how many people cannot do this. The reading of good poetry may lead you to try your hand at it yourself.

A part of every pastor's reading should be devoted to biographies, not only those of other preachers and missionaries, but of other outstanding men: philosophers, philanthropists, states-men, jurists, physicians, etc. etc.

There is also a place for the development of an appreciation of art in the pastor's life. Those who have a talent in this field will have no difficulty, but others, like me, have much to learn here. Dr. Hugh T. Kerr has developed many useful sermon il-lustrations from more or less famous paintings. Not all of us can derive the same benefit, but all of us should have at least a slight acquaintance with art.

It is best to have a set time for reading, and to adhere to it. This applies to the regular reading. Unless we have such a time we might not get much reading done. But there will often come a few spare moments and if a book is handy it is easy to fall into the habit of reading in it, often in preference to the newspaper and the news magazine.

3. *The habit of being alert.* The Lord Jesus always noticed what was going on around Him, and often what He saw served as a starting-point of His message — for example, the parable of the sower. Almost any incident, if it is carefully noted, can be of value in the work of the ministry, either by serving as an example or as a warning. Often incidents will furnish illustrations for the sermon you are working on, or for one you may wish to preach some other time. By being alert, you can collect much valuable material ahead of time.

Study your people when you are calling in their homes. Often some little thing gives you the character of the home life, for example, the kind of sheet music on the piano, or the kind of radio or television programs which the people listen to and watch. Conversation will help you further to find out where your people live spiritually.

III. SOME DANGERS

We should not close this chapter without pointing out some dangers, which may be encountered while pursuing the courses here suggested.

There is a possibility of becoming a mere bookworm, losing sight of practical things. This will be especially true if no books on practical subjects are included in the pastor's reading.

There is another danger in adopting the ideas set forth in each book read. We knew of a pastor whose people used to say they could tell whenever he had finished reading a new book by the way he preached. His sermon was colored by his reading, and sometimes the coloring met with disfavor on the part of his congregation. Sometimes it presented antagonistic views to those held by his church.

There is a further danger of too shallow reading. Let us admit that most of us would rather read something in story form than that which requires solid thinking. But the reading of some heavy books is essential to the stimulation of our thinking.

In following a well-chosen course of reading we will find a medium of self-culture and self-discipline. When a man has completed his course of training in school, there is always the danger of relaxing and becoming very unsystematic. But if his reading is wisely planned it will help him to overcome this tendency.

One suggestion we would like to leave for your consideration about systematic Bible study: It will help you in your own study to plan a series of sermons, — for example, a series on one of the books of the Bible (Matthew, Acts, Ephesians, etc.). Or have a series of consecutive topics. As a rule, you will find it easier to prepare such sermons and will not have the question every week, "What shall I preach about next Sunday?" At the same time, it will give more connected Bible study to your people, which in many churches is sadly needed.

Can you recall the names of ten books you read last year? Do you know who wrote them? What have you remembered of the theme of each book?

Chapter 7

THE PASTOR'S SOCIAL LIFE

There are good books available on the subject and every pastor ought to own and read at least one of these. In this chapter we shall look at the pastor as he appears before the people of his church and community. We do well to remember that a pastor is always in the public eye, except in the strictest privacy of his home, his study, his bedroom. But even what happens here may become a matter of common knowledge. For your character, it is best always to remember that the eyes of God are upon you no matter where you may be. For your reputation, it is just as important to remember that the eyes of the public are always upon you.

I. In The Home

We begin with the home for two reasons: (1) You will spend most of your time at home, even if you are a very busy pastor; and (2) what you are and do at home will at some time come out into the open and either help or harm your ministry. It may be possible to bluff people for a while, but not all the time.

1. *Conduct in relation to your wife.* The way you treat your wife comes in for consideration. The home life in the parsonage should serve as an example for others. It will soon be discovered if the pastor and his wife do not get along well. A pastor who had the habit of getting up first in the morning used to say that he "beat his wife up nearly every morning" until he discovered that some people took that literally. For those who understood, it was a joke, but for those who misunderstood it was a very serious matter.

Some men have unfortunately married women without any regard to their qualifications as pastors' wives. As the companion of most any other professional man, it would matter little how she conducted her home or how she and her husband got along together. As a pastor's wife, her whole life is open to the public. Both the pastor and his wife will always need to remember this.

Mr. R. was a good preacher and was sometimes invited to conduct meetings in churches outside his home community. On one occasion he brought his wife with him, which was a serious mistake. The home in which they were being entertained noticed that there were frequent quarrels between husband and wife, and reported this to their pastor. This good man in turn called on the visiting preacher and asked about these matters, for he did not believe a man was fit to preach the Gospel who did not live in harmony with his wife. Mr. R. did not deny the report but he added: "Man looketh on the outward appearance, but the Lord looketh on the heart!"

If you make it a point always to be a gentleman even in relation to your wife, every breath of scandal will be avoided.

2. *The training of your children.* This is of great importance. It used to be said that "the preacher's kids are the worst in the community." Is this true? By no means; but the eyes of the church and the community are on the pastor's children more than on any others, and if they find the pastor's children are just like the others, they are horrified. If the pastor succeeds in leading his children to a higher moral and spiritual level, the children are often avoided and left lonely, for fear they would report the conduct of others to their father. The lot of a child of the manse is in many respects quite difficult.

It has been demonstrated that a pastor's children often have a superior mentality, and that is not strange. They grew up under better cultural and educational surroundings than the average, even though their father has a lower income than most of the members of his church. Some years ago a paragraph in the *Saturday Evening Post* stated that most of the men on their editorial staff came from the manse.

At the present time, however, it seems there is a great lack of discipline in the homes of many pastors, no doubt because the parents are anxious to shield their children from being marked as "the preacher's kids." Sometimes the children resent this designation and make the attempt to hide their father's occupation. John was a Presbyterian minister's son in a small Illinois town. He came home from school one day in great indignation. The members of the class had been asked to write biographies of each other. The one who wrote John's had said: "John is a minister's son and goes to Sunday school because he has to." This caused all the indignation. In another instance, when each of the pupils in his grade had been asked to name their father's occupation, the son of a Baptist pastor had said his dad was a garage man.

There are "P. K's" today who have never been disciplined, and as a result have been badly spoiled. When they were small children, everybody in the church played with them and teased them, and the smart answers they returned were considered "cute." As they grew older they continued in the same way, but then it was no longer "cute" and "sweet"; it was obnoxious, and the same children were referred to as "the preacher's brats." The members of the church did not realize that they themselves had largely made those youngsters what they were. It is not easy to raise children in the manse. It will take a lot of strength and character to keep them from being spoiled.

On the other hand, it will surely be noticed if the pastor is too severe with his family and administers drastic punishment to them. It will be impossible to please all the members of your congregation, so the best principle to follow is the teaching of the word of God (see Ephesians 6:1-4; Colossians 3:20, 21).

3. *As a host or as a guest.* The entertaining of guests in the parsonage is worth considering. It is important to make guests feel at home, not by stiff formality, but by courtesy and politeness. It is not a mistake to have a good book on etiquette on your shelf and to read in it frequently. The essence of good manners is being thoughtful of others.

When you are a guest in a home, the rule of politeness should also be applied. Nothing that would embarrass the hosts should be said or done. Mrs. A. was a worker in a Jewish mission and made house to house calls. In one home she was given something to eat which went completely against her. It almost made her feel sick. The hostess seemed to think she had given her visitor a very special treat and the visitor dared not offend her. So by carefully not disclosing her distaste, she succeeded in not embarrassing her hostess.

II. At Social Gatherings

1. *In the church.* In the church there will be social gatherings which you are promoting for fellowship or for propaganda purposes. In such a case, plan carefully whatever you are going to do, or put it into capable hands. Be sure they are "capable." We have in mind such gatherings as a church Thanksgiving dinner, a watch-night service at which there is usually a social hour, an occasional or regular family night, etc.

If you are not promoting the meeting, let others do the planning but show your interest by helping where you can. This is especially important if some organization in the church is the sponsor. Young people particularly want to do their own planning, and resent interference by others. However, the pastor has a right to halt anything not in keeping with the testimony of the church.

2. *In the homes of members.* Members of the church should be thoughtful enough to invite the pastor to parties in their homes, but do not become angry if they fail to do so. Sometimes the slight may be intentional, sometimes just an oversight.

If you are at one of these parties, take part in all the innocent games if you are asked to do so. They would hardly play any other kind with the pastor present. And yet there are people who are bold enough to propose the playing of cards even when the pastor is there!

Care must be taken not to attempt the role of the most important person at the party. Some pastors seem to think they have to be "the life of the party" by telling the biggest jokes, or the funniest stories, or laughing the loudest at anything.

Many of the social gatherings will be in the hands and homes of young people. If the pastor is still a young man, he will not have much difficulty on this score. It is not quite so easy when he begins to show gray hair above the temples. There is a notion held by many that young people need a young pastor. This is altogether false, unless the pastor has forgotten all about his youth. We can point to large churches with many young people who are being served by older men. However, many excellent pastors have been forced to leave pastorates because of this notion. But it is true that some pastors forget their youth all too soon.

The wife of an ordained minister was being buried. He had spent many years as principal of a Christian academy. The obituary had been written by the woman's husband and went something like this: "Since we always had to deal with young people in our work, it seemed as if we would never grow old." It is important to keep your heart young to get the viewpoint of young people. Be sympathetic and understanding. If they come to you with questions or problems, be a wise counselor to them, but do not assume a "super-pious" attitude. It will help you to gain and to hold their respect. Your behavior at parties will determine to a large extent their opinion of you, whether they can have confidence in you or not.

III. AT PUBLIC FUNCTIONS

In small towns the pastor is expected to attend and even take part in many community functions, such as Memorial Day exercises, the dedication of a public building, commencement at the local high school, Fourth of July celebrations, and other patriotic or community events.

The writer had the honor of offering the invocation at a Memorial Day service in a little village in Illinois where Everett Dirksen, now United State Senator, was the speaker. When my daughter was graduated from Henry Ford Hospital in Detroit as a nurse, I was on the program to offer the invocation. The reason, of course, was because she was the only one in the class whose father was a pastor. Several members of the Ford family were present, and I was introduced to all of them. It was the most distinguished company in which I have ever been. Other pastors have similar experiences.

When present at public functions, whether as a guest or a participant, the pastor should always observe proper decorum and not attract attention to himself. In this there are many who fall down. They do what they do not want others to do. For example, they take the back seat unless they are on the program, they read something while the address is being given, or carry on a conversation with another preacher in a whisper. The latter is a very common offense and should never be practiced.

If you are invited to be the speaker at a community affair — union Thanksgiving Day meeting, Memorial Day program, baccalaureate service for the graduating class of the local high school — adapt yourself to the occasion. Try to remember that you are a servant of Christ, and at the same time the representative of the community. Do not compromise your position. Somewhere in the message, briefly and concisely, state the great fact of salvation; but do not make it an occasion for the display of your own theories or the particular doctrine of your church or denomination.

If there are other speakers on the program, be careful not to use more than your allotted time. At a Bible conference in Chicago there was a symposium on missions one afternoon. Each speaker was allowed a certain number of minutes in order to have enough time for all of them. The speaker from a Jewish mission exceeded his time by five minutes. The next speaker was from a rescue mission. He started out by saying: "The man ahead of me stole five minutes of my time. As far as I am concerned, he might as well have stolen my watch." Perhaps that remark was a lack of courtesy, but how about the guilty man? Courtesy had been lacking in him first. The eminent Hebrew Christian, Louis Meyer, used to say: "If I am told just how many minutes I have for my message I always make it a point to stop *before* the time is up. Then I am quite certain to be invited again. If people liked the address they will not say, 'It was a pretty good sermon, but it was too long.' Rather, 'I could have listened a good while longer.' " There is good advice in that.

Remember to be dignified without being painfully stiff. Some people find it difficult to strike a happy medium. They are either too formal or too informal. We witnessed the unveiling and dedication of a beautiful missionary painting in a Bible college. The artist was there to make the presentation. He did not slap the president of the school on his back and say, "Well, here it is." Instead he made a pleasant and dignified speech telling how the painting came to be and what it represented. It was brief and dignified, but not stilted.

It does not seem like proper deportment on the part of a pastor to take the part of the most ridiculous character at some community function. We knew a pastor who took the part of the "village idiot" in a community program in the village where he was pastor. Could those who had seen him thus simply erase that picture from their minds when they saw the same minister preside at a communion service, or conduct a funeral?

IV. IN THE PUBLIC EYE

We said at the beginning of this chapter that a pastor is always in the public eye. Let us emphasize that here.

1. *In conversation.* People who know are usually able to judge the extent of your culture by your conversation. Our family physician told us of having spent an evening in the home of some friends. He and the host got started talking about some events in ancient history, a subject with which both were quite familiar. But the hostess could not stand it long. She expressed surprise that anyone should be interested in what happened thousands of years ago, when they could be playing bridge instead. She was anxious to get the game started. It was not hard for the doctor to form his opinion of the degree of culture that woman possessed. People will do the same for you and me.

From a university student we learned of a woman who had come from Germany to serve on the faculty of a large university. To all appearances she was a good Christian. She told her class one day that it seemed to her as if Americans had lost the art of conversation and depended upon other media for entertainment. One of the other teachers had met her in the corridor one day and apologized for not having her and her husband in their home. She would invite them soon to a card party. The European woman thanked her and said they would be glad to come, only she and her husband did not play cards. Another wanted to invite them to a cocktail party, and she answered in the same way. Still another wanted to take them to a dance, and again she courteously declined and explained that they did not dance. Then, to the class she said: "I am sure you, like most other Americans, will feel like asking, 'Well, what do you do that you enjoy?'" She answered: "My husband and I thoroughly enjoy spending an evening in good conversation with some friends." That was a university teacher and not a pastor.

The pastor may not be the most brilliant conversationalist, but he should practice it and he *will* improve. Sometimes he may have to feel around for a while before he finds a subject on which he can converse with those present. Once in a great while he will enter a home where it is very difficult to engage the people in conversation. He may make several hopeful starts with some questions, and after there has been an answer of yes or no, silence reigns supreme again. In such cases you will just have to make the best of it that you can.

2. *In traffic.* Should a pastor obey traffic laws? By all means. Some pastors are known as speed demons. They take all kinds of liberties on the streets and highways when they know that no policeman is near. It is a reflection on their profession and brings dishonor to the Lord for a man who wears a clergy emblem on his car to be caught by an officer for speeding or some other traffic violation.

3. *In critical situations.* What we mean by this can best be made clear by means of an incident. For greater effectiveness, we let the pastor tell his own story. "The pianist in our Sunday school had told her mother that one of the high school teachers had made an indecent exposure in her presence. Her mother was up in arms about it, and soon the whole community knew about it. It so happened that the clerk of the school board was a member of our church, and the most prominent members of the church and its best supporters were close relatives of the clerk. Where did I fit into the picture? Should I say nothing lest I antagonize the most important members of my church? Should I lead in a fight to get the teacher in question ousted? What would happen in either case? This is what I did. I did not *lead* in the movement, but I had a courageous neighbor who undertook to lead in a campaign to have the teacher ousted and a new clerk elected, whose term was expiring. We drove to the county seat and obtained the advice of an attorney as to how we should proceed. A neighborhood pastor who was always loud in denouncing the evils of the community was very

much afraid of how it would affect his work, but we finally persuaded him to go along with us.

"Just how it happened I do not remember, but the school election came on a day when I was out of town. I did not try to run away but something called me from home. It had been quite an exciting day, and the board member we wanted to have replaced had been retained by a small majority. But the school board had learned its lesson. The teacher in question was allowed to resign quietly and take a position elsewhere."

The community too had learned something. They realized that their pastors were the champions of what was right, even if it endangered their own position and income.

Trying circumstances often come very suddenly and unexpectedly. They may be of such a nature as to incite us to anger and to do something rash immediately. But such behavior is a sign of weakness. A pastor who cannot control his temper loses his influence in the community.

4. *In relation to women.* Here the man who is a pastor cannot be too careful. He does not have to be a "lady's man" to be a successful minister, but neither should he be too aloof and unfriendly.

Extreme care needs to be exercised in calling where women are at home alone. It may sometimes be necessary, but every precaution should be taken to avoid misinterpretation. People will soon notice when the pastor makes frequent calls in a home where a young woman is alone all day. The calls may be perfectly in order, but the people will misconstrue his actions. There are always some in a community who like nothing better than to hear of a pastor involved in a scandal. It is almost impossible for a pastor who has once become involved ever to regain a place in Christian work. In the case of some men we know who fell in this matter, their career for usefulness in the Christian ministry was completely ruined. Dr. George W. Taft, of the Northern Baptist Theological Seminary, used to say: "A minister who failed in the field of morals cannot be trusted not to repeat the act. He should never become the pastor of another church."

We close with a verse of Scripture that has a definite bearing on all that has been said. Let us read it in several different versions and translations.

The Authorized Version: "Giving no offense in anything, that the ministry be not blamed."

The American Standard Version: "Giving no occasion of stumbling, that our ministration be not blamed."

The Revised Standard Version: "We put no obstacle in anyone's way, that no fault may be found with our ministry."

And Phillips in his *Letters to Young Churches:* "As far as we are concerned we do not wish to stand in anyone's way, nor do we wish to bring discredit on the ministry God has given us."

That is the point: Let your social life be such that the ministry be not blamed (II Corinthians 6:3).

Chapter 8

THE PASTOR'S OUTSIDE RELATIONS

Under this heading we shall discuss matters which are not exactly pastoral duties, but things which every pastor will have to meet in practically any pastorate he serves. This is true in both city and country churches. His relation to these things will probably be more conspicuous in a small town or community than in the large city, and yet there are principles that apply to both.

I. In Relation to the Community

It may be a little difficult to define the word "community" in exact terms. For our present purpose it will be sufficient to think of it as a number of people with a number of common interests living in the same general locality.

A small town with its surrounding area is usually a community by itself, though there may be some demarcations along racial, cultural, and religious lines even here.

The larger cities have suburban areas, but even within the city there are more or less distinct communities. Sometimes these fall into racial or religious groups, e. g., the Chinese community, the Jewish community, the Negro community, etc. Sometimes they represent a cultural group — the wealthier people who live in an exclusive neighborhood; groups of early settlers who were there before the city grew large; slums in which usually the poorer people live, sometimes those with questionable occupations and impermanent residence; or groups of immigrants of some particular nationality and language. But none of these actually bars others from moving in.

Each community usually has some projects that interest everyone who lives there. One author lists about a dozen such (Diffendorfer in *The Church and the Community*): town meeting (not so common any more); annual school meeting; the public school; the public library; the public art gallery; municipal buildings, parks, etc. Besides these, there are often local organizations which mean much to the residents, no matter how insignificant or even silly they may seem to a stranger who has just moved into the community.

Often there are community activities in which everybody is expected to be interested, such as local athletics; socials, parties, picnics; school dances; high school programs, entertainments, plays, concerts; sometimes even spelling bees.

The question is, how does the pastor fit into all these things? He is a newcomer and these things do not mean as much to him as to the old residents. He may be there only a few years. Should he keep aloof from everything and go his own way? That, no doubt, would be a very serious mistake. What, then, shall he do? Shall he enter into everything? Shall he try to control things which he feels are not handled right? Shall he become involved with local politics? Shall he join various organizations? Let us consider some of these things specifically.

1. *Benevolent organizations.* By this designation we refer to such organizations as the Red Cross, the Community Welfare Chest, Boy Scouts and Girl Scouts, Literary Clubs, Women's Christian Temperance Union, Veterans of Foreign Wars, etc.

No doubt all these projects have been designed to be helpful, and no doubt most of them are. When disaster strikes in the form of a tornado, flood, fire, or anything else, the Red Cross is always on the job in a short time. In a little community in Oklahoma a tornado struck at six o'clock in the evening one summer, and before it was dark the Red Cross was there to supply whatever help was needed. The Welfare Chest operates mostly in the larger cities and is designed to bring relief to those who are in need of help for which they cannot pay. The money raised goes for hospitals and other institutions, but sometimes also to the Salvation Army and local welfare agencies. The Scouts provide interesting and helpful activities for the leisure time of boys and girls to keep them out of trouble. Similar things could be said about most of the others.

Since all these agencies usually have a noble purpose, it would seem wise for the pastor to help them all he can, provided they have proper leadership. But he should always remember that his main business is the Lord's work. If he is elected to serve on a board or committee, he should accept the job, provided there are no strings attached to it. It may be possible to reach some people for Christ through these contacts. But he should be extremely careful never to compromise his own position.

2. *Secret societies, labor unions, the Ku Klux Klan.* There are others who have different opinions but it is the candid conviction of the writer that it is best for the pastor to keep away from secret societies of any kind. Twice he served as pastor of churches where some prominent members — sometimes deacons — were high-ranking

lodge members. In one little town practically every man, except the Mennonites, belonged to one or the other of two well-known secret orders. I never condemned them publicly, or even privately. When questioned about them privately, I would state my opinion. It did not take long before my stand was well-known in the community. Once my wife and I attended a supper given by one of the lodges, but it was done to avoid giving offense. One of my deacons called me on the telephone and warmly invited us. He said he would get us in his car, pay for our meals, and take us home any time we wanted to go, even if it was before the end of the program. What should we have done? We went, and thanked him afterwards, but made no other remarks. There was nothing specially evil on the program but one could easily sense the difference between that crowd and the Christians with whom we met on Sundays. There was nothing spiritual whatsoever.

The same deacon was the chief officer in the county organization of his lodge. It was customary for the organization to attend some church in the county once a year, and it would have been our church's turn that year. He mentioned this to me, but assured me that I was under no compulsion to invite them. In fact, he made it as easy as possible for me to decline, for he said if I did not wish to invite them, I would not have to give him an answer at all; there would be no hard feelings on his part. I declined by giving him no answer, and the deacon was as good as his word. He was as good a friend of mine afterward as he had been before. In thinking this over later, I often wondered if it might not have been wiser if I had invited them and preached a gospel message to them. In another church a women's lodge came one Sunday night without any invitation. They simply sent word that they were coming. The pastor did not denounce secret societies in his sermon but brought them a message from the Word of God. It was the only opportunity he ever had to speak to some of those women.

You will have to face this situation and you had better make up your mind about it. Some advocate joining at least one fraternal organization in order to have social contact with the men which might not be had otherwise. It has been the writer's experience that active lodge members, even though they were officers in the church, were never really spiritually minded men. The "fraternal spirit" seems to militate against true spirituality and has a tendency to weaken one's conviction. When a lodge meeting conflicts with something in the church, the lodge usually gets the preference.

What about labor unions? Of course a pastor cannot well join any of these; yet there used to be a laboring men's evangelist in

Detroit who held street meetings downtown every summer. He stated that he had membership cards from a great many unions. It gave him entrance to their meetings, and they respected him. On one occasion a Catholic member moved that they should refrain from smoking in any meeting at which the "Reverend Father" was present! That is more than some teachers' organizations do.

In the local church the labor union problem can become a difficult situation. The owner of a small factory had befriended an immigrant when he was a perfect stranger in this country. He had given the man employment and, since the wealthy man was a Christian, had also taken him to his church. If I remember right, the immigrant had become a member of the church himself. Then he had become a strong union man and fomented a strike in the factory of the man who had befriended him. Of course I heard only one side of the story. It might have sounded different from the side of the laborer. It would be unwise for me to jump at conclusions. But if I had been the pastor of that church, it would have been my duty to make investigations and find out the facts. And then it would have been my duty to stand by my conviction of what was right.

There is a place for labor unions. Before they were formed, many employers exploited the laborers to the limit. The laboring man was at the mercy of his employer. Now the tables have been turned. In many instances the employer is at the mercy of the union. Not all strikes are justifiable but neither are they all unjustifiable.

I became pastor of a church in which my predecessor had joined hands with the Ku Klux Klan, although it was claimed he had never become a member. The klan was strong in that community and his friendliness had brought many of them to his church services every Sunday night. But it had also split the church wide open. Some were klan members; others were bitterly opposed to it. When I came, the klan members, even those who belonged to my church, were very cool towards me. The large crowds that had come to the evening services disappeared. What should I as the new pastor do? Should I follow my predecessor's example and join hands with the klan? Should I come out and fight it boldly? Or should I keep hands off and seek to be a pastor to all of my people? The latter is what I decided to do, and the Lord blessed it. Most of my members who belonged to the klan gradually came back to the church, although one had to be patient with them. Some of them became my warmest friends. The daughter of one of them went as a missionary to India. The others continued to stand by their church and their pastor. The klan was never mentioned in my preaching; it was neither denounced nor favored in private conversation. The pastor of another church in that small town followed my predecessor's example, and the klan members other than from our church attended his church Sunday nights. I do not recall that any of them were subsequently converted and joined the church.

In my judgment it is wiser for a pastor to keep away from any organizations that seek to force any kind of religious or racial segregation. The separation from the world and worldliness is something different altogether.

3. *Community activities.* By this we refer to such activities as were mentioned at the beginning of this chapter. If they do not conflict with our activities in the ministry and do not force us to make any spiritual compromises, it would seem wise to support them. Of course it is out of the question for a true minister of the Gospel to sponsor a community or high school dance, or even have anything to do with it. It does not change the situation in the least if the dance is held in a church. The same applies to any kind of parties in which the regular playing cards are used. But athletics — baseball, football, basketball, tennis, golf — if properly conducted are worthy of support. We know of a pastor who plays golf with business men and does personal work with them at the same time. The great drawback is that so many of these games are played on Sundays. To this the true pastor will never agree. Community picnics and similar affairs will almost invariably be kept on a higher plane if the pastor participates.

In one of our communities we sometimes got together the singers from a half-dozen Protestant churches of various denominations and rendered a community Christmas or Easter cantata, which served a very good purpose. The music teacher in the high school willingly served as the conductor.

High school programs sometimes seriously interfere with the work of the church. It used to be that the church was the social center of the community; now it is the school. Perhaps the church in the past failed to provide properly for the social needs of its young people, but that is neither here nor there now. We are confronted with the fact that the school schedules its games and programs without any regard to the calendar of any of the churches. It is not uncommon for a school to have a play or a basketball or football game when the church has important meetings at which the presence of all its young people is greatly desired.

Such difficulties might be avoided if at the beginning of the school year the pastors of a community got together with the principal or the superintendent of the local school and worked out together a program with a minimum of conflicts. The sympathetic interest of the school board will be helpful, and this should not be hard to secure if they are Christians. Of course, this means that your own church program should be planned for a whole year in advance. And that is always a good plan anyway. Sometimes the necessary cooperation can be secured through the Parent Teacher Association.

Membership in the Parent Teacher Association may be very helpful. It may enable the pastor to guide to the correction of certain evils. Besides, it gets the pastor acquainted with the people of the community and also with all the teachers. Some PTA meetings quickly dispose of their business and spend the rest of the evening playing bridge. It takes a terrific imagination to see any benefit for the school children in this!

4. *Politics.* It is the pastor's duty to uphold moral principles, and sometimes he may have to take the leadership in this matter. After the death of Dr. W. B. Riley, we read a brief account of his life. It stated that some people were surprised at his active interest in local politics. He explained that it was his duty as a citizen to help make the community in which he lived a decent place to bring up his family. He was a fundamentalist and a premillennarian and had no idea of converting the whole world or making the whole world better. It is seldom, if ever, wise to take the side of any political party, unless a moral issue is involved. As a citizen, it is the pastor's privilege to go to the polls and vote. Unless he does, he has no right to find fault with the government for what it does.

5. *Christian organizations.* We refer to such organizations as the YWCA, the YMCA, or the WCTU. The first two as now generally operated are more of the nature of cultural clubs than Christian organizations. They used to be evangelical and evangelistic. The WCTU serves the good purpose of keeping the evil of liquor constantly before us. In supporting such a movement, care needs to be taken not to let its interests and activities overshadow or crowd out the pastor's spiritual ministry.

II. IN RELATION TO OTHER CHURCHES

There has been much fraternization between churches of various denominations, sometimes too much. After all, each denomination is supposed to have definite convictions about its teachings and position, and every member should know why he is a Baptist rather than a Methodist or Presbyterian, and vice versa. But it is a mistaken notion that "my denomination" and "my church" are the only right ones. If you do not agree with what your church teaches, do not try to change the church and cause a split; leave the church and unite with one with whose teachings you *can* agree.

1. *Other pastors.* It is a good policy to get acquainted with the other pastors of a community as soon as possible. According to accepted etiquette, the ones in residence should first call on the new arrival, but this is not nearly always done. Others may have failed you in this respect, but do not follow their example. Welcome the newcomer to your community as soon as possible. If you are the newcomer, you should seek to make the acquaintance of the other pastors in your community as soon as it is reasonably possible, even if they have failed to call on you first. Learn to know who they are and what they believe. Of course this should be done tactfully and without creating the impression of probing into private affairs.

Perhaps this is as good a place as any to discuss the matter of belonging to pastoral fellowship groups. In the large city there are today often separate fellowships of "fundamentalists" and "modernists." This is hardly the case in a small town. Let us suppose that you have a pastorate in a small town where there are six Protestant churches: Methodist, Baptist, Presbyterian, Nazarene, Congregational, and Pentecostal. Should you seek to have a ministerial fellowship organized if there is none? Should you join it if there is? What if you know some of the others to be modernists? What if some are fundamental but belong to denominations in which there is modernism? What if those that claim to be more spiritual are constantly preying on the members of the other churches? Such situations are not impossible. Our suggestion would be that you organize or join a pastor's fellowship, unless you are not quite sure of your own convictions. You may be able to help some of the others. We have known men who did just this.

It is the author's personal judgment that it is not necessary to limit our fellowship to those who agree in all points with us — baptism, the second coming of Christ, the relation of the Rapture to the Great Tribulation. There are true Christians who do not hold the premillennial view of Christ's return (I would not let them convert me) but who are truly evangelical. And there are still many splendid Christians in churches whose denominations are members of the National Council of Churches. While we do not endorse the Council, we would not shun to have fellowship with an evangelical pastor from such a church. The word "separation" has been overworked in some quarters and developed a lopsided application.

There are men who constantly talk "separation," but the only thing they have in mind is separation from the National Council, or even the National Association of Evangelicals. They would not dare to preach about separation from worldliness in their own churches. It is always possible to go to extremes. There are schools which make every faculty member sign a statement that he does not belong to a church that has any connection with the National Council, but they will accept gifts from fundamental churches that are included in the National Council. There is the possibility that we might become like the Pharisees, for they were the "fundamentalists" among the Jews when Christ was on earth. A true Christian, should be able to cooperate with any other true Christian, regardless of whether they believe everything alike or not.

2. *Members of other churches.* It is seldom, if ever, wise for a pastor to call in homes in which he knows the people are members of another church in that community. It may be in order in times of sickness or other emergency, especially if such a call is requested. Even then it is wise to confer with the other pastor before making the call.

It is always unethical to seek to lure people away from their own church. If they are unsaved and you wish to do personal work with them, try to do it without making a personal call in the home, Otherwise it looks too much as if you are trying to induce them to come to your church.

It is an altogether different matter if such people come to you unsolicited and desire the fellowship of your church. Even then it is advisable to contact the other pastor. If one of your members wishes to join another church, be courteous about it and release him, unless it is a cult with an unscriptural doctrine.

It will always be well for a pastor to learn just why the new member wishes to leave another church. Someone has said, " 'Spite members,' like spite marriages, do not last." The man who has had his feelings hurt by another pastor is not a good prospective member.

3. *Participation in union meetings.* At Thanksgiving or on Memorial Day it is often the practice in small towns for all the churches to unite in a union service. There are extreme "separationists" who will have nothing to do with such a service, unless the entire program is left in their hands. This looks utterly selfish. We see no harm in such cooperation. It may result in great good. It may lead people to know you who have never heard you preach in your own church. If you do the preaching, be sure to preach the Word of God. And by all means steer away from controversial

issues between your church and the others. This will not be too hard if you adhere closely to the Word of God.

Sometimes union evangelistic meetings are suggested in a community. Our advice is to participate by all means if you know what kind of message the evangelist preaches. The true evangelist will not make propaganda for any particular church or denomination. Some evangelical churches are so "fundamental" that they cannot participate in any campaign unless a man from their group is the preacher. In our judgment this is a serious mistake. Members from churches outside your own group may never have heard the Gospel presented the way it will be done by the evangelist. As a rule, your church will gain the respect of the community if you participate, and generally will also gain some new members.

Chapter 9

THE PASTOR'S RELATION TO HIS BROTHER MINISTER

Every pastor will soon discover that he is not alone in his profession. There are many other men in the ministry. In a small town there are usually three or four churches of other denominations, with pastors heading each one of them. There will of necessity be some contact with these men. Some, like Henry Ward Beecher, have thought it was not good for pastors to associate too much with each other. Of course such association can be carried too far, but there is a brotherhood of the ministry, and within proper bounds this can be a blessing. Furthermore, every pastor usually has a predecessor and a successor. The relation to these brothers is the subject we are now going to discuss.

I. To His Predecessor.

There are many men in the ministry who have never had the privilege of serving as the first pastor of a congregation. This simply means that there has always been a predecessor. I have served as the pastor of five different churches over a period of approximately twenty-six years. One was an offshoot of an emotional movement and had had only some three or four ministers. I had another church which had been served by but one man, unordained at the time, and was located in an unchurched community. This was a promising field. A fine piece of work had been done by my predecessor. Then I had a church in a mid-western state which had existed since before the Civil War. I had another church which dated from before the Revolutionary War. From this I came to a new and unorganized group in a large city, and here I had the privilege of organizing and incorporating a new church. But even here there had been a predecessor who had preached to the group without organizing it.

In the denomination in which I grew up — one of the numerous Mennonite divisions — the ministers were elected from the congregation and usually remained in the same community the rest of their life time. But even here changes have occurred and the various churches now employ full-time, salaried pastors. So, whether we like it or not, it remains a fact that with but few exceptions all of us will follow some other man. And unless we are just beginning work as a pastor, we will have served a congregation elsewhere. Those just getting into the ministry will find here some suggestions about what to do and what to avoid in relation to these others.

One important thing to remember is that every pastor has his own special group of friends, and usually also a choice list of those who oppose him. Both of these will try to get your attention. There are some who will never feel as kindly toward a present pastor as they did toward the man who preceded him. On many occasions they will speak of the way he used to do, implying that it was better than what is being done now. As a polite afterthought they may add that they like their present pastor too, but the present pastor will soon realize that he can never take the place of his predecessor in their hearts.

Then there are some who welcome the new pastor with open arms and at the very first opportunity tell him all about the faults of his predecessor. They are sure that the church now has a promising future.

Our first bit of advice is that you must never speak disparagingly of your predecessor, publicly or privately. You may have known the man and possibly realize that he has serious weaknesses, but it is not for you ever to say anything about that.

It may be that you are coming to a new field. You have moved from a distance and are a perfect stranger. Before long you will have heard things about the remote as well as the recent history of the church, especially how it fared under your predecessor. There will always be someone, it may be even a church officer, who will undertake to inform you. Perhaps he thinks he can get on your good side by telling you all the scandal about the former man. Or it may be a member who has often been in trouble with the church who proceeds to tell you all about his former troubles, for which he of course blames the former pastor. In any such case pay no heed to what is said. Out of politeness you may have to let them tell all they wish but do not let it influence your conduct. The things they tell you may not be true, or may at least be exaggerated out of proportion. Tale-bearers usually plan to put themselves in a good light at someone else's expense. Furthermore, every pastor has some good qualities, though in some they may not be as easily seen as in others. And in each church you will find some who were ardent supporters of your predecessor. You are to assume that he did the job as best he could.

Remember, too, that some day you may leave that church, and the same people who tell you about the faults and weaknesses of your predecessor will in all likelihood say the same thing about you to the next pastor.

Our second suggestion is that you do not introduce great changes immediately. If there has been a great upheaval and the new pastor is expected to straighten things out, it is a different matter. But even then you should proceed with caution.

We have known pastors to get off on the wrong foot by quibbling about the order of service. The same order may have been in use for a whole generation and a departure from it might seem to be sacrilege to some. Usually no great principle is involved. The new pastor can afford for the time being to follow the established order. If he doesn't like it, he can introduce changes gradually and tactfully. However, the pastor need not be under such domination as we once witnessed. As the guest speaker at the midweek meeting, we noticed that one of the deacons put the numbers of the hymns to be used next Sunday morning on the hymn board. The pastor called our attention to it and whispered in our ear that he would not dare to make any change, for that would cause a lot of trouble. Why should a deacon undertake to select the hymns when it is the pastor who knows what he has in mind for the service and which hymns would be appropriate?

If there are no abnormal conditions to be overcome, it is best to change as little as possible at the beginning. It will not be so noticeable that there is a new man in the pulpit. Some pastors are so anxious to impress the church with their superior leadership that they constantly call attention to the way things "are being done now." It may go over with some, but there will also be those that resent it, even those who were not on the best terms with the previous pastor.

II. To His Successor

The first thing to remember is to keep your hands off after you have left a pastorate. You may have served a church a good many years and formed many friendships among the members. Your new church is not too many miles away. At least, in our day it takes only a few hours to travel a hundred or more miles. The advice we give here is to forget as far as possible that you were the pastor of the other church, except as you have profited by your experiences there.

We knew a man who resigned from his church and went into another line of Christian work, but he retained his residence in the same city. There were several other churches of his denomination in that city, and he removed his membership and transferred his whole family to one of those churches in a different part of the city. We considered that a wise move.

We know of another man who remained within a few blocks of the church he had served but took up another kind of Christian service. It did not seem wise to move his entire family, so he merely transferred his own membership to another church. However, he took his hands off his former church completely. His wife and children reported to him how things were going, but he never sought to influence their action or tell them how to vote on any matter of church business. He remained on friendly relations with the people and also the new pastor. Even when he saw things developing which he feared would be harmful in the end, and proved to be so, he said absolutely nothing. Occasionally he visited with some of the church members, but the affairs of the church were not discussed.

Later, when the church was pastorless again, he often supplied the pulpit, and whenever the officers came to counsel with him he sought to help them all he could. When a new pastor came, he took his hands off again. Friendly relations were always maintained and they exist to this day.

As a rule, it is best not to go to a former pastorate frequently and visit among the people. Your visits may be innocent enough, but the new pastor does not know that. Besides, there will always be some who will try to tell you all the faults of the new man and his family. Some pastors are foolish enough to go back to a few intimate friends who will keep him informed about how poorly the church is doing under the new man. This is most unwise and un-Christian. We knew a pastor who had considerable difficulty in his church and, whether rightly or wrongly, he blamed the former pastor, for this man frequently came to visit his members but never called on the new man. If any visiting is done, the new pastor should be the first one on whom to call. It is even best to have no intimate correspondence with people in your former parish. It sometimes happens that a pastor leaves a church because he has been discredited or rejected by a majority. Even then he should be kindly disposed toward his successor. The new man deserves the right to a good start in any new field he may enter.

It is a well known principle of long standing that the pastor should be the friend of all of his people but be intimate with none.

This is sometimes hard to do. One is inclined to share confidences with those who seem to understand and to appreciate one's problems and to keep aloof from others. But if this principle is followed, there will not be the tendency to run back to the old friend and have the new man criticized by one of your admirers.

Something should be said about weddings and funerals in a former charge. It is not unusual for a pastor to be invited to come back and officiate at the wedding of the daughter of a former parishioner. What should he do? There are some who do not hesitate to go back for such services time and again. But under general circumstances it is wise to suggest that the arrangements should be made through the new pastor. He will be glad to transmit the invitation to the desired minister and the latter will respond to him. Unless the local minister is extremely touchy and jealous, he will be glad to fall in line with any wishes the family may have. In some cases arrangements can be made for both to have a part. In the case of a wedding the new pastor may offer a prayer and read a Scripture, or both, while the former pastor takes the vows, or vice versa. A young man who was not on the best terms with his pastor came and asked his employer in a mission, also an ordained minister, to officiate at his wedding. He accepted on the condition that the groom's own pastor should have a share in the service, and so it was done.

In one of the most beautiful weddings we ever attended the young couple came from churches of different denominations. It was a large church wedding and the two pastors had equal responsibility in the ceremony. The Methodist pastor took the vows from the groom who was a Methodist, and the Baptist pastor took them from the bride, a member of his church. Everything had been well planned beforehand and there was no confusion or any embarrassing moments.

There isn't a great deal of money in officiating at a wedding, but the pastor of a small church will often find the fee he receives will meet a particular need at that time. This is another reason why the present pastor should, as a rule, be called on to serve. Of course if this is not done, he should be just as friendly with the young couple as he was before.

The following is an extreme case, but it is true. In a certain community there lived a man who was an ordained minister. He had been graduated from college and seminary, but had never been a pastor. Becoming the husband of a wealthy woman had made it unnecessary for him to have a church. They lived on a large, well-equipped farm and he was a good manager. However, neither he nor the community ever forgot that he was an ordained minister. Often young couples who wanted to be married in a religious ceremony went to him. This put them under no obligations to any church, for often the couple feels obligated to go and hear the man who married them preach at least once. Here there was no such obligation. None of the pastors in the community liked it, but he was a popular man and nothing could be done about it. Of course the fees for such ceremonies went to a man who did not need them. As a matter of fact, this was worse than having a former pastor come in for such a service.

In the case of a funeral, the same general principle applies. It is almost impossible to decline an invitation to speak at a funeral of an older member of a former church. You may have been a blessing to him in his illness, if it was one of long duration, or he may have requested that you should have this service. However, if the thing is done properly, the invitation should come through the new pastor. Usually some arrangements can be made for both to participate, one presiding while the other brings the message. In most cases the former pastor, who has had a long acquaintance with the departed, should bring the message. It sometimes happens that an older member selects not only the pastor who is to preach his funeral sermon but also the text he is to use. Sometimes the pastor has left the church and moved a considerable distance away. The relatives do not want to stand the expense of having him come, and do not even notify him of the passing of the loved one. If this happens to you, do not get peeved.

III. To His Neighbor

Immemorial custom requires that the first visit should be made by the local people when a newcomer has come into the community. This is a courtesy that every pastor should remember in regard to men who come in to take charge of other churches in the community. New pastors have a right to expect this courtesy from the local ministry, though it is not always observed. Too many settled pastors have a tendency to become careless on this point of etiquette, but it should never be neglected. As soon as the new pastor has moved in and is settled in his home, be sure to call on him and welcome him to your community.

In a small town the other pastors are quite certain to be of other denominations than your own. You may have strong differences but, unless they represent some definitely unscriptural teaching, recognize them as the ministers of God. We heard of an extreme case where a Protestant minister exchanged pulpits with a

Spiritualist. Such of course should be out of the question. But evangelical pastors who preach the Gospel should regard each other as in the Lord.

Sometimes there is keen rivalry between two or more churches. This is not all bad but it must be kept within the bounds of Christian propriety. A little rivalry is sometimes good for the churches that engage in it, for it encourages each church to do its very best to get and to hold people; but it must always be by fair means. There is always room for all, and every Christian minister has a right to the ambition to reach out and gather all he may for the Lord without trying to take away what another has gathered.

Sometimes couples who get married come from different denominations. One may be a Baptist and the other a Presbyterian. They feel they should not be divided in this matter after they marry and must decide with which church to affiliate. When such a couple comes to a pastor indicating that they would like to join his church, it would be wise to find out if they have consulted the other pastor. If they seem to find it difficult to do so, the minister himself should talk with the other pastor to make sure that he understands the situation.

There are some people who are never happy in any church for any length of time. They move from one to another. We have heard of a church that was called "The Mad Church," for it consisted mainly of members who got mad in their own churches and joined this one. That is hardly a praiseworthy commendation.

Some of the things we have mentioned are purely matters of common sense, but it seems that in practice there are some ministers who do not display as much of that as they ought to.

CHAPTER 10

THE PASTOR AND HIS FIELD OF SERVICE

Perhaps this chapter should have had a place earlier in the book to offer suggestions to the one who is looking for a field of service for the first time. However, we are thinking also of the man who concludes his ministry in one place and is looking for another. Both of these are covered in the present discussion. It has sometimes been said that if a man is qualified and is called of the Lord, the field will seek for the man. That is not altogether true. Gideon believed in his divine call and guidance, but he also put out a fleece to make sure he was right (Judges 6:36-40).

But it is one thing to seek the Lord's will and an altogether different thing to have made up one's mind already. We are strongly of the opinion that if the right pastor and the right church get together, the result will be a long and richly blessed pastorate. The fact that pastorless churches often have numerous applicants does not violate the principle of divine guidance. Both the church and the incoming pastor should feel sure the Lord has guided them.

In the following pages we shall discuss (1) Calling a Pastor: From the Standpoint of the Church, (2) Calling a Pastor: From the Standpoint of the Minister, (3) Principles of Guidance, and (4) Details to Be Arranged.

I. FROM THE STANDPOINT OF THE CHURCH

It is a crisis experience in any church when there is a change of pastors. The former leader's ways and methods were well known; his general interpretation of the Scriptures was familiar to those who attended the services with any degree of regularity; his weaknesses and faults were understood and borne with: but the new man is a total stranger. Hearing him preach one or several sermons by no means gives a thorough acquaintance with him. Mistakes are bound to be made some time or other, but many can be avoided if the proper steps are taken before the man is called.

A church which *was* given to emotional demonstrations called to its pulpit a man who came from a very conservative background, who thought spiritual joys were too sacred to be publicly displayed. Naturally the two did not get along together. Trouble might have been avoided if the parties had known these things about each other before the man was called. In all likelihood, the church would never have considered that man.

The church should consider the fitness of the man whom it expects to call as its pastor. It should get to know just as much as possible about him, just as the bride and the groom should know each other before they get married. But even then there will still be many adjustments to be made.

Some of the desired information may be obtained from his former church, if he has been a pastor before. Schools desire to have all the information they can get before they accept prospective students. It is even more important for a church to know what kind of a man wants to become their pastor. It might not be practicable, but it seems some kind of references from his former field should be obtained. A questionnaire might be worked out and the information obtained. It should be regarded as strictly confidential by the pulpit committee. This is all the more important if the man comes from a considerable distance. It is a sad fact that some men have made long moves, at their own expense or at the cost of the church, and shortly after their arrival it is evident that the two do not fit together. In denominations where the conference or the bishop or some other board makes the appointments this will not be a problem, but even here preferences can usually be expressed.

If it is a man's first pastorate, he will most likely give the school from which he was graduated as a reference. This should always be required and will often prevent trouble later. But even such favorable endorsement is not always sufficient. Most schools try to think well of their graduates and are anxious for them to find good pastorates. Furthermore, they have learned to know the man only as a student; he may be quite different in a responsible and executive position. For such reasons a school's reference might prove to be of insufficient value. To call a new man is always more or less a risk.

The candidate's training may be a clue to his fitness. If the denomination has a Bible college or theological seminary, the graduate of such schools should have had adequate preparation. But there are also men with only the training received in a Bible institute who make excellent pastors. There have even been some without any formal education who have been eminently successful.

Generally speaking, however, the amount of training a man has should be a factor in considering a candidate's qualifications.

If the church is satisfied with the applicant's qualifications, it should make the calling of a pastor a matter of earnest prayer. If no disquieting facts are brought to light, it may be presumed that the call about to be extended is in harmony with the will of the Lord.

What we have said represents the ideal, which is very commonly violated. It is violated when the applicant is self-seeking and determined to get a certain church, whether by fair means or foul. We knew a man who took a year's leave of absence from his church to go to Europe. He left the church in charge of a friend who was to serve as pastor while he was gone. When he came back he found that his "friend" had persuaded the church to give him a call to become its pastor. In another place we knew of a man who was crowded out of his church by an assistant whom he had called because both were graduates of the same school.

The ideal is violated when the church does not properly evaluate a man's qualifications. There are churches that think more of a man's ability to draw a crowd, his intellectual attainments, his social qualities as a "good mixer," than of his spirituality, his humility, or his knowledge of the Word of God.

The ideal is also violated when the church depends on the advice of friends more than upon the Lord. Recommendations from friends may be just as misleading as recommendations from some schools.

The church should appoint a representative pulpit committee to make contact with a man who is available. In some churches the board of deacons constitute a permanent pulpit committee. It has the duty of securing pulpit supply whenever the pastor is absent, usually with the pastor's consent. If the church is pastorless, it has the responsibility of bringing desirable candidates before the church. If there is no permanent committee, it seems advisable to appoint one for the occasion with a representative from each department of the church: deacons, trustees, Sunday school, young people, music, etc.

This committee should hear the man preach in his present pulpit if at all possible, unless of course this is to be his first pastorate. If favorably impressed, the committee should invite him to preach in their church, and then let the church decide whether or not to give him a call. There should be no delay about the decision.

II. FROM THE STANDPOINT OF THE MINISTER.

It is very seldom that a man can pick the church he would like to serve, unless he resorts to unethical practices. He cannot resort to the tactics of the politician who makes great and generous promises of what he will do if elected. He must wait until there is an opening. And the opening might not be a desirable one. The man looking for his first charge usually depends considerably on the recommendation of his school, or some friend who knows of a pastorless church. The custom of making a bold application for such a vacancy used to be frowned upon, but in more recent years it has become acceptable in many quarters. We heard of a desirable church in the mid-west that was pastorless for some time and was flooded with applications. There were some thirty or more men who felt they were just the men who could acceptably and successfully fill that pulpit.

What about the pastor who desires to make a change and move to a new location? How does a pastor know when he ought to make such a change? It seems to us as if there are principally two things that lie back of a man's desire to move to a new field.

First, the Lord may open wide a door of service in another place. It may be that another church, larger, or more spiritual, or for other reasons seems desirable, offers its pastorate. This may not be too common an occurrence among small churches, but it does happen. We had a friend who during the early years of his ministry turned down many invitations from other churches. He did not believe his work was finished in the church he was serving. The invitation in itself is not proof of the Lord's call. If it were, there would only be one invitation at a time. It is necessary to give prayerful consideration to such invitations. We have known of pastors who asked the church they were serving for advice. This does not seem to be a wise procedure. There will always be some who, if any difficulty develops in the church later, will say, "We should have told him to accept the other call he had." No matter how sincere and honest the pastor is in asking for advice, the church sometimes becomes seriously divided from such a course.

Secondly, it sometimes becomes necessary to resign on faith. That brings up the question as to when such a resignation should be presented, or what should lead a man to resign when no other door of service has opened for him. We offer several suggestions.

Do not give up the work the first time any trouble develops. Young pastors sometimes sail along beautifully for the first few months in their first pastorate. The people come to hear him, the attendance is growing, Sunday school and choir are functioning properly, there is an active young people's society, and he has the respect of the whole community. Suddenly a difficulty arises. Some important member falls into sin; someone had his feeling hurt by the way the pastor denounced certain evils; someone has been slighted in pastoral visitation; two members have a serious quarrel. We have known men who under such circumstances immediately resigned. This is usually a mistake. The pastor must expect that difficulties will develop. His principal business is to preach, but he is also the spiritual leader of the flock. It is his business to seek to bring about adjustments so that the work will not be hindered.

Do not give up as soon as you find there are some members who do not like you. Perhaps they had not voted in favor of calling you. What should you do? Our experience has shown that it is best to act as if you were not aware of this situation. Call on the disgruntled persons just as you would call on friendly members. If possible, avoid talking about the difficulty, for your attitude is that you do not know of their opposition to you. But if the issue is forced, try to find out the reason for their position. Often a frank discussion will remove difficulties. If nothing is accomplished, go on just as before. It is quite likely that the largest part of the membership is on your side.

Do not give up your work merely because another church offers a larger salary and has better facilities. It is not a sign of deep spirituality to make the call depend upon the amount of money involved. Many stories have been in circulation about the pastor for whom the call to a new field was not loud enough unless it offered a certain large-sized salary. Another story tells of a pastor's son who related that his father had received a call to a better church with a larger salary. When asked what they were going to do, he said, "Dad is in his study praying for guidance, but mother has already begun to pack things." Let your prayers for guidance not become an empty form.

Do not leave your present church merely because you want to live in a college town for the benefit of your children. Of course a pastor is concerned about the education of his children. The small town in which his work lies may be a considerable distance from the nearest college. An invitation comes from another church in a town where there is a college, or where one is within easy reach. His children are just out of high school and he would like for them to go to college. The invitation has come at exactly the right time. But that is no assurance that it is the Lord's will. Circumstances like these may often *help* us to determine the Lord's will, but alone they are not sufficient.

Now for a few positive suggestions:

The time has come for a man to resign when he feels that his work in a particular field is finished. He has gone as far as he can. We knew a pastor in a neighboring city who had built up a thriving church from the very beginning. They had begun in rented rooms and had become the owners of a beautiful church building. The time came when he felt his work was done. There was no friction between him and the members, but they too seemed to think that it was time for a change. He left the church and went to a new field. The people always held him in high respect and spoke well of him after he had left.

The time has come to resign when there is sufficient opposition to hinder a pastor's ministry. There have been autocratic and ruthless pastors who removed from the church roll any members who were against them. If they had a sufficiently forceful personality they were successful with their plan. Others have tried the same scheme and failed miserably. In our opinion such tactics are not in harmony with the Christian spirit. A pastor should not act as if he were a "lord over God's heritage" (I Peter 5:3). Evil-doers may have to be disciplined, but that is not the same as excluding from membership anyone who opposes us. We should learn to work in harmony with our people just as far as this is possible. That is why the Lord put us there.

Sometimes it is the wife's health that makes necessary a change of pastorates. In some places it is a standing joke that when there is difficulty between a pastor and his people, the pastor's wife takes ill and a change of climate is necessary! It may sometimes have been used as an excuse, but there are occasions when this is a legitimate reason.

Sometimes a pastor's own health requires a change of climate. He may be incapacitated much of the time where he is but is assured that in another climate this difficulty will not bother him. In such a case it would seem that the Lord is speaking through circumstances.

II. Principles of Guidance

On the part of the church, Dobbins mentions ten principles that should guide both the church and the pastor Gaines S. Dobbins, (*Building Better Churches,* Nashville, Tenn.: Broadman Press, 1949, p. 314). We adapt only five for the church and four for the pastor. Some apply to both.

(1) The church should not be pressurized by influential recommendations. It should be ready to receive recommendations, but must come to its own conclusions upon investigation.

(2) The church should know a man's record before making any specific approach. This will make it necessary for the pulpit committee to make very careful investigation.

(3) No man should appear before the church as a "candidate" whom the committee would not recommend. He might be a good preacher and make a good impression on the church, but the committee might know something about him that would make him undesirable.

(4) The church should never have a long list of "candidates" whom it will hear before extending a call. It might be that the man is sacrificing an opportunity elsewhere to appear in this particular church. He may be without a church, especially if he is just out of school, and it may be necessary for him to know the church's intentions immediately after he has been there. Action should be taken by the church right after hearing a man. If more than one is heard, it is quite possible that each one will have found some supporters and, on later occasions when there is tension or friction, someone will say, "I always thought we should have called the other man."

(5) It should not be necessary to mention this but it is very important: the church should ask and look for divine guidance. This should not be an empty form but a sincere seeking after God's will.

Some of these suggestions on the part of the pastor are positive and some are negative.

(1) The pastor should always be concerned about the welfare of his church. It should come ahead of personal considerations. This is a high ideal, but a pastor should have high ideals, above those of other men. He should not look for another field until he is sure his work is done in the old. There are several criteria by which this may be determined. One is whether or not souls are being saved through his ministry. Another is whether the audiences are increasing or decreasing in number. A third, whether or not the members of the church are growing in spirituality.

(2) The pastor should not misrepresent himself, his education, or his qualifications. If he has attended a school but not graduated, he should state the honest facts. If he has never studied Greek or Hebrew, he should not try to create the impression that he has. There is an amusing story about a ministerial candidate who appeared before a congregation of whom he had heard that they

liked men who sounded scholarly, even though their own educational level was not very high. He knew only the English language but he went to work and spelled some long words backwards (garbage-can; cannonball; moccasin) and inserted them in appropriate spots in the sermon. The scheme worked. The people thought he was repeating in Greek or Hebrew what he had just said in English. He got the church! Of course no one ever did exactly that, but there are always among us some who like to create the impression that they are highly educated men when they are not.

(3) The pastor should not resort to "wire-pulling" through influential friends. Such procedure might get him the call, but surely such a man could not expect God's blessing upon his ministry.

(4) This is a repetition of the last principle given for the counsel of the church: seek the will of God in prayer. If the church prays for divine guidance and the prospective pastor does too, you can expect the Lord to hear and answer. How will you know that it is the will of God? A number of things may enter in. You may be properly qualified and have received a call. The church may be offering you a larger salary and better facilities. There may be a college near the church where you could send your children. But these things are not enough unless you have a deep conviction that all of this is of the Lord. *Do not accept the call unless you have this conviction.*

We repeat that all of this is highly idealistic and perhaps some of the details have never been followed, but we are strongly of the opinion that not so many ministers would seem to be misfits if these principles were observed.

IV. Details to Be Arranged

These are things that ought to be attended to when the call is extended and accepted. It is a poor policy to leave this until a later time. Some churches are very parsimonious, and some pastors are inclined to make excessive demands.

1. There should be a definite arrangement of the term for which a pastor is called. There are some churches that have fallen into the habit of calling a man for just a year at a time. The call has to be renewed at every annual meeting. It makes it impossible to do any long-range planning of the program of the church. And it might have a tendency to influence the pastor's method of dealing with church problems. However, some arrangement should be made about the length of service. The church constitution may have provided for this, but if not it should be taken care of. It seems best to call a pastor for a term of mutual agreement. If the

pastor wishes to resign he can do so, and if the church wishes to make a change it should have the right to do so. There should be an agreement of how much advance notice must be given in such a case.

2. The amount of the pastor's salary should be settled when he is called. The pastor should not be greedy, but the church should be conscientious enough to pay a salary which will enable the pastor and his family to live in keeping with the times. Too often the pastor's wife has had to pinch and scrape to make ends meet. She should know how to economize, but it should not be necessary for her children to be constantly dressed in made-over clothes discarded by the wealthier members. It should also be stipulated as to when the salary is to be paid, whether weekly, semi-monthly, or monthly. For modern times the weekly pay day seems the best. If living costs rise, the church should make a commensurate raise in salary and not make it necessary for the pastor to ask for more. But if incomes all around are decreasing, the pastor should be willing to take a cut in his salary.

3. The pastor's residence should be arranged for at the time of accepting a call. Where there is a parsonage there is no problem. Where there is no parsonage, the church should help the pastor find a house and either pay the rent or add sufficient to his salary to enable him to do so. In these days of income tax, money allowed for housing is not taxable.

4. The pastor's moving expenses should be paid by the church. A timid man may be afraid to ask for this, and there are churches that will allow him to pay out of his own pocket when he is scarcely able to do so.

5. Another detail to be arranged is the pastor's vacation. There was a time when it was deemed that pastors should always be on the job because "the devil never takes a vacation." If the pastor's vacation means that there will be no services during his absence, something is out of order. The work of the church must go on, but the pastor needs a change once in a while. Some still argue that the apostles were always busy and never took vacations. They do not mention the fact that there were other things they did or omitted which do not serve as patterns. For example, none of them traveled by train, an automobile, or an airplane. If the people say it is because times are different now, we answer that they are different in other respects also. Some churches provide for the pastor's vacation in their constitutions. This should be inquired into and arrangements made if not provided for.

In the same connection, we mention absences from the pulpit

during the year, attendance at conventions, etc. If the pastor for some reason must be absent for a Sunday, it should be determined beforehand who will pay for the pulpit supply—likewise, if he is absent for a conference or convention in the interests of the church. The thoughtful church will see to it that these things are not an extra expense to the pastor, not even his traveling expenses.

The thing most needed by any man is the loyal support of the whole church. Of this he should be assured when he assumes the pastorate. Sometimes he is told he will find a united church to stand by him, but after a short time he discovers that the membership is hopelessly divided and there is constant friction between two or more groups. We have said that churches should get all the information they possibly can before calling a man: let us say now that the new pastor (or perhaps we should say the "candidate") should obtain all the information he can about the church which may become his future field of work. If he knows where the weak spots have been in the past, he may be able to steer past them when they show up during his ministry. If he does not know about them, they may precipitate trouble.

Dobbins says: "The visiting minister should make it clear throughout that favorable replies to his inquiries will in no wise be the condition of his consideration of the call, but that he is simply seeking clarification to the end that he may have a more intelligent basis for his decision, should the call be extended" (*Ibid.*, p. 310).

CHAPTER 11

PASTORAL CALLING

By "pastoral calling" or "visitation" we refer to the calls a pastor makes in the homes of a community with spiritual ends in view. Notice that we do not say they are calls made in behalf of the church. It is quite certain that the church will benefit as a result, but the primary reason for calling should be a desire to be of spiritual help to someone. In the church of a small town it may well be that most of the calls will be made in the homes of members in order not to encroach upon the field of a neighboring pastor. In the larger city it may embrace all the homes in a community except those that are definitely settled in another church. It also includes calls in hospitals and, if necessary, in jails. Since it is a part of his business to bring comfort where it is needed, he should not avoid any place where he might be able to bring spiritual help.

There is a tendency among some recent seminary graduates to try to run a church from an office, even a small church. They insist upon having all the most modern equipment in their office and bombard their membership with frequent letters and circulars. This will never take the place of calling. It is still true that "a house-going pastor will produce a church-going people."

I. On Whom Should a Pastor Call?

All the church members need pastoral care, but some need it more than others. The following list may not include each and every case, but it conveys the general idea.

1. *Those who are sick.* There is scarcely ever a time when there isn't someone sick, even in a small church. Some have illnesses of long standing, others have been suddenly seized. The sick people always have the first claim on the pastor's call. Jesus said, "They that be whole need not a physician, but they that are sick" (Matthew 9:12). This is true spiritually as well as physically.

The sick always have the first claim on the pastor's time. True, sometimes he does not know about a member's illness for several days. The people in the home call the doctor to come and minister

91

to the sick; they expect him to come, and he does. They do not call the pastor, but they expect him to come just the same. They go on the assumption that he will find out in some way. Often they are highly offended if he does not find it out and does not call. Efforts should be made to instruct the church along this line. The pastor is there to minister, but he cannot minister unless he knows the need.

2. *Those who are in trouble.* Every Christian at some time passes through a crisis experience. It may be an accident, a sudden illness, an unexpected bereavement, a financial distress, an emotional upset, or a threatened mental breakdown. Such experiences drive some people to acts of desperation. Some say nothing about their troubles, and only a few call on the pastor for help. As a rule this does not apply to the sick and the bereaved. But even then some of them never let the pastor know.

It will be a little easier if some of the facts are known. But infinite tact will be required to deal with such a situation. Each case will be different and it is impossible to lay down an infallible rule of procedure. Christian people need to be reminded of the sacred vows they took. They should be shown what the Bible teaches about the relation between husbands and wives. Wise. counseling and prayer may prevent the wrecking of a home.

3. *Those who are lonely.* It has sometimes been said that a large city can be a very lonely place for one who has come from the country or small town. But the country or small town can also be very lonely for one who grew up in the city. In most cases these lonely people are strangers who have just come into the community. The pastor should make it his business to find such strangers, make them welcome, invite them to church, and see if there is any service he can perform for them. It is not wise to make a call while the household goods are still being unloaded from the van, but do go as soon as the people are settled. Most newcomers will resent the intrusion of a visitor while their furniture is in disarray.

Another class of lonely people is found in the widows and maiden ladies who live alone. They should by no means be neglected, but extreme care needs to be taken in making such calls. A warm friendliness is in order, but extreme care should be used to keep within proper bounds. Someone in the community will soon notice it if the pastor makes frequent calls in a home where a woman lives alone, or is at home alone all day with no one else in the house. His visits may be perfectly in order, but the appearance is not good. And any community scandal can wreck a church, or bring an untimely end to a pastor's work. It is best if the pastor's wife or one of his children accompanies him on such calls. If he is an unmarried man, the danger is even greater and it is impossible to lay down a hard and fast rule. Some places may have to be avoided altogether, or it might be possible to make the visit in the company of a friend.

Undue familiarity with women is always out of order. In more than one church there is a woman who has designs on the minister. He will notice it by the way she looks at him, the way she holds his hand in hers after shaking hands, or by the fact that she writes him frequently, or sends gifts to him. As a climax will come an invitation to call. Sometimes even a married man is approached in this way. The wise pastor will know what *not* to do.

4. *Those who are discouraged.* Various experiences can cause discouragement. It may be the business failure of a prominent man in a small town. He may have been inexperienced and not wise in management. It may even be that he failed because some church members did not pay their accounts. We have known such things to happen. In one instance a filling station burned down in which many well-to-do farmers had charge accounts. The records burned with the building and we learned later that only one of the debtors ever called to make settlement. The young owner was forced out of business. Such experiences are very humiliating. Thoughts of self-destruction sometimes come to such a man. He feels thoroughly disgraced. He may spend many sleepless nights trying to figure out what to do. If the pastor calls on him, speaks words of encouragement to him and prays with him, the burden usually becomes lighter.

A farmer may be discouraged over a crop failure. The wheat was just about ready for harvest when a sudden hailstorm destroyed it all. Or an early frost, or a drought caused a complete failure. Some become antagonistic toward God through such experiences, for they believe that God is back of the weather. A young peach grower lost his entire first crop through a heavy frost. As a result he dropped out of church. After a few Sundays the pastor called on him. "Do you think I could love a God who takes my entire peach crop away from me?" said the young farmer. "God is more interested in raising men than in raising peaches," said the pastor wisely. It helped the farmer to learn an important lesson.

5. *Those who are bereaved.* This applies whether or not death has been expected or comes suddenly. News of a member's death may reach the pastor five minutes after he has come home from calling on that member. He should go back immediately. People

are very appreciative of a pastor's thoughtfulness in such a case. No attempt should be made to arrange for the funeral at this time, but speak only words of sympathy and comfort. There may be too much excitement and confusion to read from the Bible and pray, but you can at least quote a few appropriate words from the Bible.

6. *The members of the church.* In a small church the pastor should call at least once every year in the homes of all his members. In the big city church this is impossible. Other persons than the pastor take care of the visitation. In the small church no one should be neglected by the pastor. He will need to call on people of various occupations, different states of health, varying cultural levels, in homes that are kept neat and orderly, and also in homes that are just the opposite. He no doubt will find places that he prefers, but he should practice impartiality. However, if some need more pastoral care than others, these are the ones who should receive it — the aged, the sick, the dying.

It is a good plan to divide the parish into sections and announce on Sunday, or through the bulletin, that in a certain week you will be in one particular direction from the church, in another week in another. Most people will make it a point to stay at home, or tell you if they cannot be at home. We knew a city pastor whose people sent word through the maid that they were not at home, unless he had made a definite appointment to call at that time. This hardly ever happens in the country. If there is any danger, telephone ahead that you are coming.

7. *Unchurched people.* Every pastor has the right to call on people who have no church membership, at least not in the vicinity. But should he call in the homes of people who are members of other churches in the community? As a general rule, we would say that it is best to stick to his own people and the unchurched. But what about people in whose churches the pastor is not preaching the Gospel? It is difficult to give a categorical answer. If a pastor knows of unconverted people in other churches, he may feel a strong urge to call on them and seek to win them for Christ. It would seem that courtesy demands he should get in touch with the other pastor first. If the other pastor is so "liberal'" that he is not concerned about the salvation of his people, it would seem right to make a call, but he should make clear from the beginning that he is not trying to win a new member for his church but is solely going as the messenger of salvation to a needy soul. We are aware that even this will not save him from unjust criticism, but there are times when the duty is so clear that it cannot be re-

fused. This is especially true if the individual is lying on a sickbed, and even more so if the patient has called for the pastor. It is best to bring such cases before the Lord in prayer and to await His guidance.

8. *Those who are in prison.* The prisoner may be a church member, for even such sometimes fall into deep sin, or it may be someone from the community who has no church connection. He should be sought out and an attempt made to show him a better way. He may never have gone to any church, but a kindly visit from a pastor at such a time may kindle his interest. Even if he does not receive you kindly, it will be worthwhile to make the attempt. As a rule it will also increase the respect of the community for you. Jesus said: "I was in prison, and ye came unto me" (Matthew 25:36). Let us not think that prisoners are too far away to be reached for Christ.

II. The Elements of a Pastoral Call

There are men in the ministry who have a natural talent for visitation. To such it is hardly necessary to lay down any principles of procedure. Others find calling a difficult responsibility. I must confess that I belong to this group. What I have learned from my own experiences should be helpful to those with a similar handicap.

1. *The time for calling.* It used to be a custom that a pastor spent his forenoon in the study, his afternoon in the field visiting among the people. Today some have no calling program at all, others do some calling but have no regular program. It is proper to spend the morning in the study. Two sermons and a prayer meeting message have to be prepared. The careful pastor, even though he has served other churches and has many sermons filed away, will never go into the pulpit without careful and fresh preparation. The one who is serving his first pastorate will soon discover that he needs to study if he wishes to bring helpful messages to his people.

To go calling in the afternoon will produce variety and relaxation. This will be refreshing. To bend over books constantly will tend to produce a "bookish" preacher. What he says may be philosophically correct, but it does not reach the people where they live. For this he needs personal contact with them. And only visitation provides this contact.

Calling should be done in the afternoon because the average housewife has finished putting the whole house in order by that time. She does not like to have the pastor come when the dishes have not been washed and the rooms not put in order. No calling should be done on Saturdays, which is house cleaning day. Of course there may be some exceptions.

Another reason why the afternoon is best for calling is the fact that the children will be coming from school, and the grown-up children from work. The pastor should make it his business to know each child by name and have something to say to him. Every member of the family should know him and regard him as a friend.

2. *What to do when calling.* The author's father was not a minister but he always had something to say when he met people. For some this is much more difficult. The pastor who does not have this natural ability should cultivate it. Says Harmon (*Ministerial Ethics and Etiquette,* p. 89), "It should be the aim of the pastor to make himself a part of the home while he calls, but at the same time guard his own essential character." He should be able to adapt himself to each home in which he calls. If he is at ease and the conversation comes naturally, if he can show a genuine interest in things he sees without prying into anything, if he can talk intelligently to the children about their school work, if he can ask intelligent questions about the husband's employment of which he may know nothing, the family will soon begin to feel as if they "have known him always." This is a high compliment for any minister. However, the pastor must not demean himself but always remember that he is a servant of God. Cheap or questionable jokes should never fall from his lips. He should never speak disparagingly of others. Nor should he ever engage in gossip about other members. A mistake here may have far-reaching results.

3. *How long to stay.* The length of a call will depend upon its nature. Is it a "professional call" or a "social call"? We once knew a worker in a Jewish mission who reported having made 1200 calls in one month. He was a student in summer school at the same time. Those calls must have been extremely brief and perfunctory.

By a "professional" call we mean one that is made solely as a part of the pastor's work. Calling is expected of him, and he tries to make as many calls in a day as he can. But most such calls have a tendency to become stereotyped. The pastor enters, greets the people, takes the seat offered him, asks a few questions about the spiritual condition of the people, offers a brief prayer, and is on his way again. Such calls may occasionally be necessary when he is pressed for time. As a rule they do not create the right impression. This is especially true if there are unsaved members of the family present. The impression is created that all this is done because it is the pastor's job. He calls because he gets paid for it. The people do not learn to know or appreciate him. Such calls can be made in ten or fifteen minutes.

In a "social" call the pastor comes as a friend. He is not in a hurry and takes time to talk about the family, about their occupation, and things of general interest to them. His conversation puts them at ease. If he is tactful, he will get the people to do more talking than he does. But he must never forget that he is the servant of the Lord. He must not depart without talking about spiritual things. Often such a call affords an opportunity for counseling.

We knew a pastor who enjoyed being invited out for Sunday dinner. He felt he could get much nearer to his people than in any other way. There was nothing to rush their conversation. Often he would learn of needs he had not known existed. Furthermore, by finding out where people lived spiritually, he knew what kind of messages to bring to them.

Calling in a hospital must of necessity be more or less professional. A pastor is permitted to make calls at any time, if he makes known that he is a minister of the Gospel. But it is wise to abide by visiting hours, unless there is an emergency. If he has to make frequent hospital calls, it is wise to get acquainted with those in charge and to respect their wishes. By no means should he ever sit on the edge of a patient's bed. If there are visitors present, there is a danger that the patient will be forgotten in the conversation. A hospital call can usually be completed in fifteen minutes. It should not last longer than half an hour.

Should prayer always be offered in the sick room and in the hospital? Circumstances will determine this. Some patients suggest it, others may wish it but be too timid to mention it. They are disappointed if it is not done. However, care should be taken in how one prays. Unless the patient has been told that he will not recover, it does not seem wise to mention death. Pray for his recovery instead. This and a word of cheer are often a help to the patient and speed his recovery. Be sure you do not pray too long. Be brief and to the point. We once heard of a man who prayed all around the world at a sickbed and when he finally stopped he found a patient had died. When he expressed surprise at this, the nurse said, "No wonder you did not notice it, for you were in India at the time."

What about if the patient is unsaved? He might not say anything but quite often such a person is surprised if you do not pray. At the bedside of an atheist, we asked permission to pray, and it was granted, although not very enthusiastically.

We close with this final remark. If you are called to be a pastor, your principal work will be that of preaching, but the very next to it will be that of getting to know your members by calling on them and keeping in touch with them.

CHAPTER 12

THE PASTOR AND THE SUNDAY SCHOOL

It is well to remember that the Church existed a long time before the Sunday school. Perhaps the Sunday school as we know it today was not necessary in apostolic days and in early centuries of the church. Much of the preaching was teaching. The sermons of the apostles recorded in the New Testament are all of the teaching type. This is also true of the preachers of the early centuries. Men studied the Scriptures very carefully in order to ascertain the exact meaning, and this they passed on to their people. It is different in many churches today. No Bible teaching is given from the pulpit. Instead, the pastor chooses a few words from a verse of the Bible, perhaps with a striking statement from which he derives a topic upon which to discourse.

Is the Sunday school still necessary today? The above paragraph answers the question. There is very little teaching in the average church aside from that given in the Sunday school, and often that is very weak. A few years ago we talked with an evangelist and he told us that at the time the Sunday school was "the pastor's biggest headache." It may be better now since a revival of interest in the Sunday school has taken place. The great national conventions held in recent years have done much to reawaken interest.

There are still pastors who have no adequate idea of the place of the Sunday school in the program of the church. It is a time-honored custom in America to have a Sunday school in every church, and so they follow along that line. On one occasion a pastor was on the program for a paper on "The Workers' Meeting." He talked about everything else. Seemingly he had no conception of what that subject meant. He treated it as if it referred to a meeting in which the pastor taught the Sunday school lesson to all of his teachers in advance of Sunday.

In the author's library there are quite a number of books on Sunday school organization and operation, but not one of them makes any mention of the pastor. It almost looks as if he is not needed.

I. THE PASTOR'S PLACE

It should be remembered that the Sunday school belongs to the church, and not the church to the Sunday school. When you see the bulk of the Sunday school—children, young people, and even adults—leave the church after Sunday school, with only a handful left for the worship service, it almost looks as if the church were a small branch of the Sunday school. The Sunday school is a very important part of the church, but it is not independent of the church, unless there is no church organization. The American Sunday School Union and some other associations are doing a notable work by establishing Sunday schools in unchurched areas. As soon as possible, a church should be organized and assume control over the Sunday school.

At the head of the Sunday school is the Superintendent. While this is not a book on Sunday school methods, a few words are in order here. If the church sponsors the Sunday school, there must be some definite connection between the two. This is accomplished if the church elects the General Superintendent. In a small church he would be the only Superintendent. There are some who think that the Workers' Council, consisting of all the officers and teachers, should have this responsibility. Others believe that the church should elect all the officers. We believe it should at least elect the Superintendent. He is the connecting link between the school and the church.

It is the responsibility of the church to support and, if necessary, finance the school, and not *vice versa*. This does not mean that we should take no offerings in the Sunday school, or ask the school to help with financial projects such as missions, building programs, etc. Let it do all it can. It is a good way to teach children to give. But in the final analysis, it is a church project and the church is under obligation to maintain it.

We include here a word about the length of the Superintendent's term of office. In a large church there would be an Educational Director, but in a small church the entire burden rests on the Superintendent. He is usually elected for a year at a time. In exceptional cases the same individual may serve in this office for many years and do much to build up the school. But too often such an individual gets into a rut and chokes the Sunday school. There comes to mind an old lady, the wealthiest member of the church, who had been Superintendent for many years. Her usual procedure was as follows: after coming to church she would find a hymn book and select the opening hymn. This would be followed by "repeating" the Lord's Prayer. There might be another hymn and some announcements and the "preliminaries" were over. Seemingly she gave no thought to the Sunday school until she got there Sunday morning. Needless to say, the Sunday school was not in a thriving condition. To the lady's credit it must be added that she stepped aside graciously when a successor was elected.

While the Superintendent is the organizational head, the pastor is the spiritual head of the Sunday school. His counsel should be sought by the Superintendent and all the workers. He is the man who has training, or should have, and his counsel is usually valuable. Of course in some places this is not desired. There are always some people who know everything better, whether it be in the Sunday school or any other matter. Sometimes it is not easy for the pastor to gain the proper control. This is true especially if the school has existed independently, or has been accustomed to acting independently of church or pastor. It may require a great deal of tact and patience to get it to take its proper place.

The same thing is true of organized classes. These can be a great help to the church and the pastor under proper leadership. Otherwise they may become a great hindrance. It sometimes happens that such classes act as if they were responsible to no one. They make plans without considering anyone else in church or school. If there is no other way of solving the difficulty, it may become necessary to dissolve such classes. This should be avoided except in extreme cases.

But coming back to the pastor, he should always be in the Sunday school regardless of whether he teaches a class or not. He should know each teacher, and, unless he teaches a class himself, occasionally visit each of the classes so he will know what is being taught. In a small church the pastor should know every man, woman, and child who are members of the school. Unless he does this it will appear as if he is lacking in interest, and how can he expect others to be interested?

II. THE PASTOR'S ACTIVITIES IN SUNDAY SCHOOL

This raises the question as to whether the pastor should ever serve as Superintendent or not. We would say that as a rule this work should be left to someone else. Situations may exist which make it necessary for him to take this office. One such is if no one else is qualified. This is more likely to happen in a new work than elsewhere. In order to keep the work going in the best way possible, it may be necessary in the beginning for the pastor to serve as Superintendent and guide the Sunday school.

It may also be necessary when a situation exists that needs

correction. In a certain church a condition existed which made a drastic step necessary. A new pastor had been called and he soon found that the Superintendent was the "boss" of everything. Neither the church nor the new pastor wanted this to continue. So the pastor prevailed upon the church to let him superintend for a while. When things were going properly, another man was elected to that office. By this strategy, serious trouble was avoided.

The pastor should understand the organization of the Sunday school. Seminary trained men have no difficulty here, but there are still some who have never studied the subject. They may go to conventions, and then come home and keep on doing just as they have done in the past. In my contact with several hundred churches, I have found some pastors who had no idea how a Sunday school should be graded. Many knew nothing about graded lessons. Of course such schools were ungraded, and in some all the classes still studied the same lesson. The pastor should know how to grade a Sunday school properly, even if no one else does. For even in small churches the school should be graded. It is also wise to use a good series of graded lessons. We go on the assumption that those who read this book will know about these things. If not, be sure to get some good books on the subject.

While much of the pastor's influence will be behind the scenes, he should be prominent enough so everyone in the Sunday school will know who he is. This should not be difficult in a small church. However, we know of one small church where one of the little girls thought the Superintendent was the pastor, largely because the pastor had no part in the Sunday school.

There are some differences of opinion as to whether or not the pastor should teach a class. In our opinion he may do so, although this depends on circumstances. If there are enough qualified teachers, there is no reason why he should first teach in the Sunday school and then also preach in the morning services. It will conserve his strength for his main job.

If the pastor teaches, he is usually given the Adult Bible Class. This is natural, for he is the one best acquainted with the Bible and best able to explain its meaning to the adult mind. He should be able to arouse interest in Bible study. We have known pastors who built up a large church membership by developing the Bible class. However, we would suggest that if he has a qualified teacher the job should be left to him. It will be good for the teacher, the class, and also the pastor.

There are instances in which the pastor is better qualified to teach some other class. Some make excellent teachers for young people. Such a man does not necessarily have to be young himself. If he has gained the respect of his young people, he can lead them on to a serious study of the Bible. We know of one pastor whose young people became so interested in Bible study that they met with him on a week night to study New Testament Greek! And this was in a small church. Another pastor conducted a class which finally dropped down to two teen-age girls. And they never forgot that their pastor had been willing to go to all that work for just the two of them.

In some cases the pastor has a special talent for dealing with Intermediates, or even some other class. If possible, he should have the class for which he is best fitted.

If he does not teach regularly, he should always be willing to substitute if it becomes necessary. The school should know that it can always count on the pastor.

The pastor is the ideal man to teach the Teacher Training Class. Yes, even small churches should have such a class. It is appalling to discover how many teachers there are who have no training. They do their best with the knowledge they have, but undoubtedly they could do much better with adequate training. If no such class exists, the pastor will do well to organize one. Most demoninations now have such courses. But if not, or if they are not satisfactory, excellent material may be obtained from the Evangelical Teacher Training Association (Chicago). This class may be held during the Sunday school hour, but we believe it is better if there is more time for it, say a fifty-minute class period. Such a time could best be found on a week night. Sometimes Sunday afternoon is suitable.

If the church is small enough, the pastor may combine calling for the Sunday school with his regular ministry of calling. However, it is better if the Superintendent or the teachers do the calling on behalf of the Sunday school. But it will still be well for the pastor to know if the people in a home in which he calls are regular in Sunday school or not. This applies alike to adults and children, for both should be in Sunday school.

The pastor should have a part on every special Sunday school program. Sometimes he is asked to bring a message at the end. In such case the pastor should be wise and make the message as brief as possible. No lengthy address should be attempted at the close of the Christmas or Children's Day program. A brief word would be in order, but it should be made interesting. If the pastor has no part, he should at least offer a prayer at the beginning or at the end.

Chapter 13

THE PASTOR AND CHURCH MUSIC

For most of us, it is impossible to think of a church service without music. Whether there was any singing in the apostolic churches we do not know for certain, but we are convinced the early Christians knew how to sing. When Paul and Silas had been put into the dungeon of the prison at Philippi, with their hands shackled and their feet fast in the stocks, they "prayed, and sang praises unto God; and the prisoners heard them." If they had not been accustomed to singing under other circumstances, they would not have been able to sing then.

The idea of singing in worship may have come to the Christians from the Old Testament. The book of Psalms is the great hymn book of the Bible. David was a musician and played the harp; we do not know whether or not he was able to sing, although he is called the "Sweet Singer of Israel." He certainly wanted others to sing. The Psalms are the lyrics for the singing of the temple choir. They are full of the praise of God. There are some Christians today who think we should sing nothing but the Psalms and not make any use of "human hymns."

There are still some people who look upon a song service as the "preliminary part" of a service. This is an outrage. Granted that the sermon is the main feature, it should never be forgotten that the music is an essential part of the service. Since singing always precedes the sermon, it really takes the lead in worship. This is one reason why a pastor should have some acquaintance with music. In a large church there may be expert musicians to take care of that department, but in a small church it may all depend on the pastor.

I. Congregational Singing

Since this forms an important part of any church service, we speak of it first. A good many churches may not have a choir, but they all have congregational singing.

Is a song leader necessary? In our opinion the morning service in a small church is more devotional without a man standing at the front and waving his arms. The hymns used are all well known, and it is enough for the pastor to announce the hymn and to start each stanza simultaneously with the piano or organ. In some old-time German churches they had a "Vorsaenger," a man who knew all the tunes and always started a song. This was also the time when the minister would "line out" the hymns. That is, he would read a line, which was then sung by the congregation. Then he would read the next line, and so on through the entire hymn. The "Vorsaenger" would always be the first to start each line.

At the evening service it is well to have a song leader, if you can find one who is capable. But it is altogether possible that the pastor will have to do his own leading. In order to do this properly, he should have some knowledge of music.

What are some of the qualifications of the song leader? We mention the most important ones. First of all he should be a Christian. He should of course be able to sing, but it is even more important that he should be a Christian. We cannot imagine an unsaved man leading God's people in worship or singing gospel songs that invite the sinner to accept Christ.

Then he should be able to sing. He may not have the trained voice of a professional soloist, but he should have a good, clear voice that can be heard all over the sanctuary. There may be rare exceptions to this where a man is able to get good singing from a congregation without being a good singer himself. The general rule is that he should be able to sing himself. We should add here that some women make very good song leaders.

The song leader should have a pretty good knowledge of music. At least, he should be able to read music to the extent that he can learn a new song without difficulty. Unless he has this ability, he is bound to get into a rut and sing the same songs over and over again until the congregation is thoroughly tired of them. We have known men who were good Christians and good singers, but who failed at this point. They had no ambition to improve their knowledge of music and to learn new songs.

He should know how to interpret hymns and gospel songs. It is not necessary to try to make an audience sing like a trained choir, but one should know the difference between a prayer, an invitation, and a cheerful testimony. It is the duty of the song leader to put this across. Dr. D. B. Towner, who was for many years music director in the old Moody Church, Chicago, was an expert in this field. His audiences soon learned to watch him and to follow his direction. They would sing fast or slow, loud or soft, as he directed them. They learned to stop long enough for rests and to prolong a hold as long as he indicated.

It is not always easy to find this kind of leader in a small church, which again makes us say that the pastor should have some ability along these lines. Occasionally a pastor does good work who has no singing voice and no knowledge of music, but such a man is the exception and not the rule.

Now let us give some thought to the type of hymns and songs to be used. Perhaps we should point out that generally speaking hymns are poems that are directly addressed to God in praise, prayer, or worship. For this reason it is advisable to use hymns in the morning service and gospel songs in the evening service, which is usually more of an evangelistic nature. We have heard of a pastor who had his congregation sing "The Church in the Wildwood" at a morning service!

There are many kinds of hymns suitable to a service of worship. Most denominational hymnals have excellent selections. The topical index in such books is a good guide to the contents of its hymns. Some hymns are full of devotion and adoration, such as "Jesus, the Very Thought of Thee," "Still, Still With Thee," "Sun of My Soul," and many others. Some are primarily worshipful, such as "Holy, Holy, Holy," "May Jesus Christ be Praised," "How Great Thou Art." Inter-varsity publishes a small book of "Hymns" most of which are devotional and worshipful. Then there are hymns of the Christian life, setting forth the conflicts, the joys, and the victories. Others deal with Christian service and consecration. The pastor should know how to select hymns which will be appropriate for the sermon he intends to preach. This is why he should select all the hymns for the morning service. Greater latitude can be given to the song leader in the evening service.

The hymns used should be doctrinally correct, although it is not necessary to be too squeamish. Occasionally it may be well to suggest the change of a word or two to bring the hymn nearer to our conception of Christian truth. For example, the words "I'm the child of a King" are more definite if made to read "I'm *a* child of *the* King." Our Christmas carols contain a good many unscriptural phrases, but they have long been a blessing and there is no harm in using them as they are. For example, "We Three Kings of Orient Are" — the Scriptures do not call them kings nor do they say that there were three.

If possible we should see to it that the hymns we use are literarily correct. This is usually above question in the standard hymns of the church, though poetic license has led to some ungrammatical expressions such as, "We've no less days to sing God's praise than when we first begun." Also, in our opinion it is a poor usage of the English language to address the Lord as "Thou" in one line and familiarly to call Him "You" in another.

Hymns used should be musically correct. There is no question about this in denominational hymnals, but it is different with some of the gospel song books. Some of these songs have been dashed off quickly without much regard to laws of harmony. The congregation should be taught to appreciate and recognize good music whether in song or chorus.

The song leader should determine the manner of singing. There are congregations that spoil the grand old hymns by dragging them to death. On the other hand, there are some who drive them to death. We were at a Student Volunteer Band meeting where the precentor whipped the congregation through every hymn and song no matter what its contents. The song leader should also keep in mind that loud singing is not necessarily good singing. We believe much can be done to train congregations to better singing either through the pastor or a good song leader.

In the evening there is usually a song service at the beginning of the meeting. Somewhat lighter music than the staid church hymns is in order. Of course nothing frivolous should ever be introduced. The songs used should be mostly gospel songs. It is not even amiss to have songs that contain the gospel invitation in the song service. They help prepare the way for the evangelistic message which usually follows. And they are appropriate even if the message is of a different character. In this song service it is proper to introduce some choruses, but be sure they have a real message. This is also the right place to introduce new songs. Most audiences enjoy the learning of a new song every once in a while.

There is much room for the improvement of congregational singing, and pastors can do much to bring this about.

II. The Church Choir.

The church choir has often been called "the war department" of the church. But as Dr. W. B. Riley says, there is no need for this. Musicians are just like other people and should be dealt with as such.

Every choir needs a director. Sometimes the directing can be done by the pianist or organist; sometimes there is no one else to do it but the pastor. The author does not claim to be a singer or a musician, but he has pastored several churches where there would have been no choir if he had not conducted it.

The qualifications of the chorister should be the same as those of the song leader. He should distinctly be a Christian. Large churches sometimes hire expert musicians regardless of whether they are Christians or not. This is a serious mistake. In a small church the choir director usually comes from the congregation, or at least from the community. This is all the more reason why he should be known as a Christian.

He should also definitely be a musician, at least, he should have some talents along the musical line. The more training he has, the better it is, but such men are not easy to find in a small church. He should be a man who is not satisfied with what he knows but should constantly seek to improve his musical education. If he is competent in music, his organist and choir will have confidence in him. It will be possible to learn and to render anthems and cantatas of a high quality.

The pastor should be able to tell when the music of the church is good and when it is bad. He should be able to judge the quality of the performance of the choir.

Small churches depend upon volunteers for membership in the choir. In every congregation there are men and women who can sing well and of these the choir should consist. In our estimation it is best to have a choir of young people, though it is not always possible to find enough of them. But in many places, even in large churches, some members have continued in the choir until they were in the seventies. Not all singing voices last that long.

Should all the choir members be Christians? Preferably, yes. The praise of God from the lips of the unsaved has no value. And it sounds incongruous to have them sing songs of invitation to the unsaved. There are possible exceptions. Also, those who sing in the choir are always there to hear the sermon. Often in evangelistic meetings such people have been among the first to get saved.

Of course those who wish to be in the choir should have a good voice. It is not always wise to extend a public invitation to those who wish to sing in the choir to come to choir practice. There are some who do not know they cannot sing. It is better for the pastor or chorister to solicit members individually after he knows something about their voices. In this way it is easier to keep undesirables out.

Choir members should have some ability in reading music. We have known of good singers who failed at this point. Even some renowned public singers have confessed that they always had to memorize the music they were going to sing. It is much easier to learn new pieces when the singers are able to read their parts and will not have to depend on the piano or organ. Of course they should be able to stay on pitch. We knew a man who was good as a soloist without accompaniment. He could not keep pitch. Of course he could not sing in a choir or a quartet.

If you have capable singers, use them occasionally to sing solos. The pastor's wife or daughter does not necessarily always have to fill this role. If she does, the people will depend on her, or get tired of her. Nor should members of the pastor's family serve as pianists or organists if there are others in the congregation who are qualified. The more you can get members to do these things, the better it will be for the church.

Choirs should be well-trained in the singing of hymns. Do not take for granted that because a hymn is well known the choir will know how to sing it. We once heard a college male chorus do an abominable job of singing "What a Friend We Have in Jesus." They had sung special numbers well but evidently had neglected practicing this one because "they all knew it." It is well for the pastor to have selected his hymns before choir practice night, and for the choir to go over them since the choir leads in the congregational singing. The choir should also be taught new hymns and songs before a congregation is asked to sing them.

It has long been the custom for choirs to sing anthems. Occasionally objections are raised because the music is too difficult for the average congregation to follow. This can be overcome by using simpler ones in the beginning. There may be anthems with an inferior content, but quite often they contain the very words of Scripture. For this reason we heartily endorse their use.

For special church seasons such as Christmas and Easter, it is well to choose a good cantata and have it sung at the evening service. There are pastors who do not agree with us. They think every service should have a sermon. It seems they have not noticed that a good cantata is sometimes as good as several sermons, for it brings the Christmas or Easter story in a most beautiful way.

If there are not sufficient voices for a full choir, there are usually enough women to have a two-part choir with anthems arranged for soprano and alto. These can be obtained from Christian music publishers.

There is a place for all kinds of special music in the program of a church, such as male or female quartets, girls' trios, duets, and solos. The church is indeed blessed that has such talent and it should freely use it. Often it will help secure loyalty to the church. This is especially true of young people. But we heard of one church which had a male chorus consisting of men who had gray hair. This was one qualification for membership. All had been singers in the past. It was known as "The Silver Men's Chorus."

In our estimation, it is good to have a "song service" once a month. At this meeting the song service is longer than usual and there are several special numbers by the choir and possibly by quartets, trios, etc. The sermon of necessity has to be shorter than usual. When such song service nights become known in a community, they will help to bring in outsiders.

We also believe a Christmas Midnight Sing could well be fitted into many church Christmas programs. Here again the choir and other groups take the lead. But there should also be a good deal of congregational singing. Such a service would not require any sermon.

There are wonderful possibilities for a church in the field of music and the wise pastor will seek to develop these.

CHAPTER 14

THE PASTOR AND MISSIONS

The words "mission" and "missions" have a variety of meaning. Primarily, the thought of the fulfillment of an errand underlies all of them. In the terminology of Christians, the thought is usually that of bringing the Gospel into all the world. This includes "home" missions in one's native country, and also "foreign" missions in other parts of the world. We use the words in this chapter as referring to the program of world evangelization with emphasis on work in foreign countries.

We once knew a man, a professing Christian and church member, who used to say that after his farm was paid for and he had erected all the necessary buildings, he might be able to give something for missions, but not until that time. Many churches are like him. They are not opposed to missions but they are not primarily interested in them. The expenses of the local work are always thought of first; then if anything is left, something might be done for missions. Some books on pastoral theology teach the same thing. We believe there should be a place for missions in every church program. Large churches can usually do more than small churches, but we believe no church is so small that it could not do *something* for missions.

The pastor is the natural leader in this program. It is a good thing to have a Missionary Committee, but as a rule the committee will accomplish little or nothing unless it is led on by the pastor. This is the reason we devote a whole chapter to this subject. A missionary-minded pastor will as a rule produce a missionary-minded church.

I. THE PASTOR SHOULD HAVE INFORMATION

The pastor should be the best-informed man in the church on the subject of missions. Here we have sometimes discovered a discouraging lack. Some pastors know that Africa is a mission field, but they know very little about its many countries, varieties of people, differences of climate, etc. This is more than discouraging — it is tragic.

Men serving in denominational churches usually have had a course in denominational missions in college or seminary. Courses in missions are now offered in all Bible colleges and institutes. These should give the pastor a *start* in the study of this important subject. Too many let it go at that. They took the subject because it was required in the course, not because they were interested in it. Confessions of students have shown that they were in the class only because it was required for graduation.

The right kind of pastor will keep himself informed even after he has been graduated and is in charge of a church. Seldom will a church prosper the way it should if it is not interested in missions. And very rarely will the church be interested if the pastor is not.

It is easy today to keep informed about missions. Denominational journals bring reports from the places the denomination occupies. Practically every independent mission publishes a monthly or bi-monthly magazine with stirring reports of the work done on its fields. Individual missionaries send out prayer letters informing their mailing list of blessings and disappointments in their experience. Other Christian magazines usually have a department devoted to missions. In recent years even leading secular magazines from time to time have brought lengthy articles about some thoroughly evangelical missions. There is no reason why a pastor, of all people, should not have up-to-date information about missions.

In addition to the information obtained from literature, the pastor should have personal contact with missionaries. This is not difficult either. There are always missionaries on furlough from all parts of the world. They are not always within easy reach of the church in a small town, but the pastor can meet them at conferences, fellowship meetings, and other meetings of Christian workers. Here he has the opportunity of learning first hand what is going on in the mission fields today. He should make use of this information in his preaching and pastoral work.

II. THE PASTOR SHOULD IMPART INSTRUCTION

The church that is ignorant about missions is to be pitied. Most likely it is the pastor's fault, for he has not instructed them. He should gain all the information he can for himself, and then present it to his people to give them missionary interest.

Such instruction can be given by preaching. According to our observation, many today preach series of sermons. This is good. At the end of a series, before beginning a new, bring a strong missionary sermon. Some have such a sermon once a year, but that is not enough. Even a long series can sometimes be profitably interrupted with a sermon on missions. It will provide variety.

In addition to this, some missionary thoughts may be included in almost any sermon, for the Bible is a missionary Book from beginning to end. Ofttimes illustrations from the lives of great missionaries serve to drive home a point in the sermon. At the same time, they can be used to call attention to missions.

Some churches have the good custom of observing "Missionary Sunday" the first Sunday of every month. If your church did not have it when you became pastor, you should introduce it. On this day there should be a brief message on missions in the Sunday School and the sermon should be a missionary sermon. The pastor himself can bring the message, but if he does so he should be full of up-to-date information about conditions on various fields, or on one field in particular. If possible, it is best to secure a missionary on furlough for the message, even if he is not from your church or denomination. We have found that people are far more interested in experiences on the field, stories of conversion, progress of national Christians than in the political situation of any country.

Talks on missions can also be given at the weekly prayer meeting. A good plan is to take one field about once a month and give a brief survey of it. Use slides or moving pictures if you can obtain some. People always like to see pictures. They make the work of missions more real to them.

Missionaries can be used on any Sunday. Some pastors do not like to give their pulpit to anyone for a Sunday morning service. In our opinion, no harm is ever done by this. It is not quite so easy to get them in a small place, but if you keep your eyes open, it can be done. We have been surprised sometimes when my wife has been asked to help find a speaker for a missionary banquet in a church with which she had no connection. The pastor should have had such information.

One of the finest things for a church missionary program is an annual missionary conference. The entire responsibility for such may be too heavy a load for a small church. Then it is advisable for five or six or even more churches in adjoining neighborhoods to unite in such a program. Meetings during the day can be held in the largest or the most centrally located, and a speaker can be in each of the participating churches at night, speaking in a different church each night. In this way some six fields or missions can be represented, no speaker will be idle any night, and each participating church will derive benefit.

In connection with such a conference, the children should not be forgotten. One of the five or six missionaries will surely be qualified to speak to children, possibly more than one. Such meetings may result in the call of some of the boys and girls to go to the mission field. Attractive missionary tracts should at this time be put into the hands of the children. The author has been interested in missions from childhood. The most interesting speakers for me always were returned missionaries. Then, in the Sunday school, missionary tracts were often given to the children at Christmas time. The time to interest people in missions is when they are still young.

Some churches have an annual missionary banquet for which they secure a dynamic speaker, usually a missionary on furlough or a missionary secretary. We believe this is a good custom. There is the danger of people thinking more about the food and the other parts of the program than about missions.

III. The Pastor Should Practice Intercession

Quite often we put prayer last, even pastors. We say, "Well, if we can't do anything else, we can pray." That makes it sound as if prayer were our last resort. We should think of it much sooner. The fact is, we should pray *first*. This is true of the pastor's relation to missions.

He should pray for missions in his private prayers. It is a good thing to have a prayer program that takes you around the world in a week. I have used the following schedule for a good many years: Monday: Africa; Tuesday: China and Chinese people all over the world; Wednesday: India and Southeastern Asia; Thursday: Roman Catholic countries and Communist countries; Friday: the islands of the world; Saturday: the Jews and the Indians; Sunday: pastors, evangelists, and other Christian workers. If possible, have something specific to pray about each of them.

The pastor should pray for missions at the weekly prayer meeting. At most such meetings the opportunity is given to make special requests for prayer. Unless he has someone else to do it, the pastor should offer specific prayer requests for missions. He may have some recent information about a crisis, about a great need, and he should bring this before the congregation intelligently so that he and they can offer prayer. No prayer meeting should be held without some prayer for missions.

There should also be prayer for missions in the pastoral prayer on Sunday morning. That pastoral prayer is a very important part of the service. More people are present than at the prayer meeting and all the congregation should unite with the pastor in the great petitions he offers. Pastoral prayers contain many elements, but they should not be too long and should be right to the point. Missions should never be left out.

IV. THE PASTOR SHOULD ENCOURAGE MISSIONARY GIVING

We have heard of pastors who are afraid to encourage giving for missions because they fear it will curtail their salaries. This may or may not be true. A man as selfish as that should not be in pastoral work. But as a matter of fact it has been demonstrated that as a rule the church that gives liberally for missions will not forget its own pastor. There are some exceptions to this, and such congregations should be taught their responsibility with relation to the pastor. Galatians 6:6 teaches that he who has been taught in the things of God should not forget to support the one that taught him.

Denominational churches often have a quota assigned or suggested to each local church as its share in the denominational missionary budget. This quota should always be within reach of the congregation. Sometimes large quotas are assigned with the expectation that they will not be met, but they are made large so that some effort will be made to reach them. It is thought that more money will come in this way than if a smaller quota is assigned, which will not be met anyway. Of course ofttimes larger quotas could be met, and would be if properly encouraged, but we believe it is wiser to make it small enough so you will be sure to meet it and then "go over the top." That is much better than to lag behind.

All churches, whether denominational or independent, large or small, should have a missionary budget. We knew a church that gave nothing for missions except the money that came in the birthday bank in the Sunday school. But it called a missionary-minded pastor, and before he left it had a missionary budget of $1500 a year. Later it undertook the support of a full-time missionary.

The missionary budget should be adopted by the annual business meeting and if possible should be covered by pledges from the members. It may be wise sometimes to accept a budget higher than that for which there are pledges in order to encourage faith and to challenge the people to more prayer and giving. The pastor should set the example in giving.

Independent churches will mostly support independent missions. But even here there should be a budget, and it should be determined what amount each of the missions it helps support should receive. If there is any doubt about any mission, let a representative come and answer questions about it.

It is a blessing for a church to undertake to support at least one missionary. Larger churches can support more, but one may be enough for a small church. It stimulates interest in giving if the people know the individual for whom their gifts are being raised.

V. THE PASTOR SHOULD ENCOURAGE MISSIONARY GOING

We have left this to the last because it is the most important. It is possible to produce not just one but a number of missionaries in one small church. We know of a small church in a small town which produced a large number of missionaries and other Christian workers, mostly under the ministry of two or three pastors. They had the vision and were able to impart it to their young people.

This encouragement can be given from the pulpit. References to missions in sermons should not refer only to praying and giving, important as they are, but should have a definite challenge to young people to dedicate their lives to the Lord. The pastor can do this if his heart is in missions. In addition to this, missionary speakers are helpful in presenting such a challenge. Every young Christian should consider carefully whether or not God wants him or her on the mission field. We know that not all are called, but each one should make sure of the will of God for his or her life. The reason why false teachers and misfits get to the field is because many who were called did not go.

This encouragement can also be given in other ways. One of the pastors of the above-mentioned church always had an ardent desire to go as a missionary himself. When the Lord did not lead him that way, he did his best to encourage other young people to go. He did this by personal words, but also by missionary instruction. Not only did he often have missionaries come to his church, but he organized a class for the study of missions. The young people of the church who were interested met on a week night and studied an up-to-date book on the subject of missions.

We firmly believe there will be more spiritual life in a church that prays for missions, gives for missions, and furnishes young people for missions than in one that is concerned only with its own progress. The pastor who does not encourage missions is failing in his ministry.

Chapter 15

THE PASTOR AS COUNSELOR

By "counseling" we do not mean merely the giving of advice on certain occasions. A high school graduate might seek the pastor's advice as to the college he should attend. A sick member, especially if he is new in the community, might ask for the name and address of a good family physician. Occasionally a member who is about to purchase a new car might ask the pastor's opinion about the make of car he thinks best. There are other occasions when people might seek the pastor's advice or opinion. But this is not counseling. By counseling we mean that people who are confronted with serious problems are led to seek out the proper solution.

Counseling has always been a part of the pastor's ministry. Jesus counseled with Nicodemus and led him to see his need of the new birth. No doubt Peter and Paul and the other apostles counseled with people who came under their care. Down through the years of the Christian Church, every pastor has dealt with the problems of some of his members. In recent times this has been given more emphasis. In bygone years not much was said about this phase of pastoral work. It was done as occasion arose without talking about it. It was not always of the best quality, but often resulted in the solution of serious difficulties. In our day whole books have been written on the subject. We advise the young pastor to get one of the several books.* But always remember that if the book was not written by a Bible-believing Christian, it will not get at the real spiritual problems which bother many people. Unbelieving counselors and psychiatrists may instead do a great deal of harm.

More people need counseling than ever before. Popular magazines have sections devoted to counseling. In the cities there are professional counselors. Many of these serve a very useful pur-

*An excellent one is *The Psychology of Counseling*, by Clyde M. Narramore. Grand Rapids: Zondervan Publishing House, 1960.

pose. But there is a phase of counseling which can be properly done only by a Christian. Sometimes individual Christians have a special talent for this work. We know a devoted Christian woman who has a master's degree from a state university who had no special training for this line of work but who had been successful in dealing with many who were in great difficulties. She testifies that she has always been successful if the counselee had ever learned to know Christ as his Saviour.

I. People Who Need Counseling

There are any number of classifications into which people who need counseling may be divided. Some writers list as many as fourteen, others ten. Because of our space limitations, we try to group them into just four.

1. *The spiritually needy.* First of all, this refers to those who are unsaved. True, not many will voluntarily come to the pastor and seek counsel. Some personal work to show them their *need* may have to be done first. But if there is even a little interest, the wise pastor will often find a way of making the path of life clear. Some are perplexed about God's wisdom when they see the evil in the world. Some are afraid of hell. Some know they are lost but blame other Christians. All these and many more need more than to be told to be born again.

Those out of fellowship with God on account of sin are another group. No matter what the sin that brought them out of fellowship, they have continued in sin and now feel that they are lost. Perhaps they were never saved in the beginning. This should be investigated, and the way of salvation pointed out. If they were saved, they need to be shown that the way back is the way of confession.

Then there are the discouraged, those who lack assurance, people who are new in the community, those recovering from serious illnesses. Practically all of these are in need of spiritual ministry. Some may consult the pastor with their problems, but some may have to be sought out if one wishes to help them. The pastor should be on the alert to discover them.

2. *Those who contemplate divorce.* That the divorce rate is constantly on the increase is a well-known fact. It is quite common even among professing Christians. Even in small churches one often finds divorced people. Not much can be done after a divorce has been granted. The time to deal with people is before that time. A good time to begin is to counsel with young people before they are married. Some ministers will not officiate unless they have previously counseled with the couple. This should always be done

if they are members of the church, and it should not be neglected with outsiders who come in to get married. Wise counseling may help start a happy marriage which will not end in the divorce court.

It is not always easy to see where there are marital difficulties. Often the pastor knows nothing about them until he hears rumors. A series of sermons on the sacredness of marriage might prove helpful. It might lead one of the couple to confide in the pastor. This will be easier than if he has to probe into their private affairs — most people resent such intrusion. But if confidence has been gained it will be easier to frankly discuss their problems with them. Speak to each one separately at first and then both at the same time. Many difficulties can be ironed out in this way and divorce prevented.

3. *Disturbed people.* By this term we refer to people who have mental or emotional disturbances. The whole field of psychiatry deals with such people. It is very important that an understanding, spiritually-minded minister should deal with them, especially if they are Christians. Non-Christian psychiatrists often take the Bible away from the patient. They blame it for causing the disturbance. Christian couples who have sought such help have sometimes been led to a dissolution of their marriage.

In our opinion, many who are patients in mental hospitals are there because of spiritual problems. Sometimes they are unsaved and under conviction of sin. Sometimes they are under great strain because of some secret sin they have committed. Sometimes they are filled with fear because of conditions in the world. Sometimes they are maladjusted to society. For most of these the Chirstian minister has a remedy which physicians and psychiatrists do not possess—namely, the consolation that comes from the Word of God.

4. *Quarreling members.* The best of friends sometimes get into a quarrel over a very trivial matter. Other church members find out about it and soon it is the common property of the community. Usually members of the church take sides in these matters, some with one and some with the other. If nothing is done about it, a serious church quarrel may develop. It is advisable for the pastor to get the two with whom the quarrel started to meet with him and discuss the whole matter frankly. Most likely it will be discovered on which side the guilt lies. The guilty party must also be led to see it. When this has been done, a thorough reconciliation should follow. Do not forget to pray before you part. It might also be well to declare before the whole church that the difficulty

between these persons has been settled and that there should be no further talk about it.

Many other and unexpected problems may come up for solution. The pastor should rely upon his personal knowledge of God and His Word and his understanding of human nature to guide him in all his counseling.

II. Principles of Counseling

Some specific suggestions have been given in the previous section; here we shall give some general principles for guidance in counseling.

1. *The right attitude.* This is very important. If the counselor has the wrong attitude, the counselee will build a wall around himself which it will be impossible to penetrate. One should be very careful not to cause needless offense. However, it may become necessary to make some shocking statements to get the counselee to see himself as he really is.

The counselor should be *very attentive.* He should not look bored or disinterested. Usually the counselee will be quick to detect lack of interest and will refuse to go on with his story. He wants help and that can come only from one who takes pains to understand him and his problems.

To be properly attentive may require considerable *patience.* We have known pastors who would listen to only half the story and at once proceed to give advice. In most cases the counselee will be too timid to insist upon saying all he has to say. If the counselor had heard the whole story, his counseling might have taken a different direction. So be patient and hear the entire story, no matter how long it takes. This is very important, for you cannot get to the bottom of any case unless you know the whole situation.

Above all be sure you are *sympathetic.* Do not assume a "holier than thou" attitude. It may be helpful to admit that you have gone through the same experiences and have been attacked by the same temptations. This will often startle the counselee, but when he sees that you have shared his experience he will be more willing to confide in you.

Do not be shocked by anything that is confessed to you. There are some who like to shock the pastor and there are others who think their case is so desperate or so evil that such a man as the pastor will surely be shocked. Give no indication that what is being confessed is altogether unusual. Christ as our High Priest is "touched by the feeling of our infirmities; but was tempted in all points like as we are, yet without sin" (Hebrew 4:14). He is not shocked by any temptation we may have nor by any sins we have committed. He knows all about them. The wise counselor will acknowledge that all such things are common to man.

What goes on in the counseling room should be a matter of the *strictest confidence*. We knew a man who drew from his son's young wife the confession that she had been indiscreet before her marriage by assuring her that what she told him would remain between them and God. But in a short time the whole community was talking about it, and the poor girl almost lost her mind. A pastor who betrays confidence once will never be trusted again in the same community. Some pastors' wives cannot be trusted with such confidential matters. Every pastor should know his own wife.

2. *The right solution.* It is usually in order to end a conversation with prayer, but not always. A young fellow came for counseling about the liquor habit. He had grown up in a Bible-believing, Bible-preaching church. He knew all the right answers. The first time he came, he confessed that he was under the influence of liquor and that for him to pray would be hypocrisy. The counselor agreed with him. He came a few weeks later and this time he agreed to have prayer. He himself offered a simple prayer. It would have been unwise to press it upon him the first time. However, there are others who come with the hope that the pastor will pray with them. They may not mention it, but will be greatly disappointed if permitted to leave without prayer.

It is always in order, we believe, to suggest the reading of certain passages in the Bible. The pastor who is acquainted with his Bible will know what passages to suggest. It is best not merely to say, "Read your Bible." Most people will not know where to begin. Often other Christian literature can be recommended. Every pastor should have some books on his shelves that he can lend to those who need their message. Even here he may mark certain passages. In subsequent counseling he should find out whether or not the selections from the Bible and other literature have been read, and what has been the counselee's reaction to them.

Sometimes one consultation will be sufficient. More often it will take a number of conversations. It is not enough to get the counselee to see where the trouble lies, and that is where some counselors end. The remedy must also be worked out, and that can only be done through the Word of God and prayer.

III. Precautions for Counselors

In his endeavor to help in the solution of problems, the pastor should be very careful not to do the wrong things or speak the wrong words. If he is not careful, he may do great harm. He should know enough psychological principles not to harm anyone.

The counselor must remember that he is *not a physician.* In the pioneer days of our country, the minister was often the best-educated man in the community. People came to him for help of all kinds. Sometimes he had some simple medicines which he prescribed for certain ailments. Under the blessing of God, these were often helpful. It is different today when it is illegal to practice medicine without a license. Besides, mental illnesses are of such a nature that a careful examination is necessary. Pastors have offered medical advice with disastrous results. It might be advisable to confer with the physician and to seek to cooperate with him. Many physicians have a low opinion of the clergy and their ability to give any advice in the treatment of mental ills. Conferences with them might convince them otherwise. This alone would be a victory. But furthermore it would help both the physician and pastor to understand the condition of the patient better and to enable them to work together for his benefit.

Sometimes it may be necessary to consult a psychiatrist. But we again caution against sending anyone to a psychiatrist who is not a Christian. He has no understanding of spiritual problems. You can fully cooperate with a Christian psychiatrist. But do not try to pose as a psychiatrist. You will find that many cases can be solved by pastoral counseling and prayer.

The counselor's attitude should be so friendly that the visitor will not feel embarrassed to speak very freely. If possible he should avoid embarrassing questions. Yet these may sometimes be necessary to enable the inquirer to see himself clearly and what has caused his problem.

Great care should be taken not to give occasion for anyone, especially woman counselees, to give *false reports* about what happened at the interview. There are women who like nothing better than to involve the pastor in embarrassing situations and then to bring false accusations against him.

Nor should anything be said in the counseling room *about others who have come with problems.* Most people think their problems are unique and that no one else has ever faced them. Under such conditions it might be well to refer to others but in such a way that their identity is not revealed.

It is almost impossible to avoid *cranks* and those who drop in for "just a minute" and stay on and on. If a crank catches you "in" unaware, deal with him courteously and as briefly as possible — likewise with those who stay on and on. Kindly inform them that your time is limited and perhaps you could meet again soon.

Do not forget to pray about each individual case in addition to the prayer you may have had with them. Counseling needs much guidance from the Holy Spirit.

CHAPTER 16

THE PASTOR AND HIS YOUNG PEOPLE

Do young people still go to church? There are millions in the United States who have never darkened a church door, millions who have never been to Sunday school. It may be they have been prejudiced against the church by their home environment. Or they may be ignorant of what the church is and teaches because they have never attended one. It is also possible that no one in the church has sought to interest them or to offer a program that would attract them. It is not true that the preaching of the whole Gospel will fill the church with young people, nor is it true that preaching a modernistic doctrine will drive young people away from the church. In either case, it requires something more than the message of the preacher to reach them.

In my experience as pastor, I took charge of one congregation that had in it married people and children. There was no "middle class" of young people. The work had grown up around a Bible teaching ministry addressed to the adult mind. The children had come along with their parents. It took some time for those children to grow up, but they did. And once we had produced a "crop" of our own, it was not so difficult to bring others. Young people will draw young people, regardless of the age of the pastor.

It is sometimes claimed that young people will not come unless there is a young pastor. That is not altogether true. Dr. George W. Truett pastored the First Baptist Church of Dallas, Texas, until he was an old man without losing his young people. The same can be said of Dr. A. B. Simpson of the Christian and Missionary Alliance and others. But a young man is often an attraction. And yet sometimes he is so immature that old and young alike lose interest in him.

In the average small church there will be found a group of young people. There may not be many, but it will be worth the pastor's effort to keep those he has and to seek to bring others. He should make sure they are Christians and then interest them in the Christian life and service.

I. WIN THEM

The fact that young people come to Sunday school and church does not prove they are Christians. Some of them may have been baptized as infants or in very early childhood, which likewise does not prove they are Christians. They may be members of the church without being born again. The wise thing to do is to get well acquainted with each one of them. This is not very difficult in a small church. Through contact with them, it is usually quite easy to see whether they are really saved or not. If they are not saved, do not antagonize them and drive them away from the church, but seek to show them what they are missing. To some extent this can be done by preaching evangelistic sermons, but in a great many cases the approach will have to be made personally and privately. If they respect you, this should not be too difficult. Let them see in your own life that a true Christian is a cheerful person and that there is joy in following Jesus. Carefully avoid creating the impression that you are so much better than they and that you are "talking down" to them. Magnify Christ and what it means to be a Christian. Challenge them to undertake that which may seem difficult, but which can be done with the help and power of God. Your church will have no future unless it can win and hold young people. In the light of this, it seems strange that some books on pastoral theology say nothing on the subject and that some pastors cater to the older people in their congregation and neglect the young until they lose them.

But it should always be kept in mind that to fill your church with young people will have little or no value unless you win them to Christ. Then secure their loyalty to Christ and the church.

II. INSTRUCT THEM

It is supposed by some well-meaning Christians that to win young people for Christ is sufficient. They do not need any human teacher; the Holy Spirit will teach them all about Christian living. True, the Holy Spirit is the best Teacher, but He makes use of human beings and human means. The apostle Paul led many people to faith in Christ and did not let them go as soon as they were saved. The record of His work in the book of Acts and the writings in his epistles are proof of that. The new-born soul is something like the new-born babe. Life is there, as well as the instinct to preserve it and the desire for food. But there are a great many things the child has to learn before it will be a mature and independent adult. So it becomes very important to instruct young people in Christian living.

To some extent this can be done in the regular preaching services. However, it is not necessary to select popular subjects for discourse and to neglect the Bible. It is very interesting to note how the apostle Paul proceeded in his epistles. There is usually (except in Galatians) a doctrinal section in which he points out all that we have in Christ, and how we have obtained it. Then follows a practical section on how Christians ought to live in the light of all this. And in this section we find all the instructions we need for Christian living, both from the negative and from the positive standpoint. We have known Christians who believe you must never tell a Christian that there are certain things he cannot do. Just show them what they have in Christ and what they can do and they will forget all about the other things. This was not the view of Paul. He says: "Walk not as other Gentiles walk" (Ephesians 4:17). "Be ye angry and sin not: let not the sun go down upon your wrath" (Ephesians 4:26). "Let him that stole steal no more: but rather let him labour" (Ephesians 4:28). "Grieve not the Holy Spirit" (Ephesians 4:30). "Let all bitterness, and wrath, and anger, and clamour, and evil-speaking, be put away from you" (Ephesians 4:31). And in the fifth chapter of the same epistle he uses many more negatives about fornication, uncleanness, covetousness, unfruitful works of darkness, drunkenness, and many other things.

So do not be afraid of the negative. But do not forget the positive. This is very important. Paul also knew this, for along with all of his negatives he gives splendid positive instructions. Instead of walking as Gentiles, we should have Christ as our example. Instead of stealing, we should earn our living. Instead of using foul language, we should speak words of helpfulness. Instead of anger and bitterness, we should be kind and tenderhearted. Instead of becoming drunk, we should be filled with the Holy Spirit. The best program would be to preach a series of sermons on the epistles and point out all they teach about the Christian life.

Sometimes such a series can be used to advantage in the prayer meeting. It might help bring young people to this meeting if they knew they would hear something of practical value to them. Such talks should not be boring but brief and to the point.

To quite an extent this instruction can also be given in personal counseling, which we have discussed in a previous chapter. Keep in mind that young people will not come to you for counseling until you have won their confidence.

Youth meetings can also be helpful in teaching about Christian living. Be sure you get speakers or lesson material that show an understanding of the young people of today. It will not be necessary to lower any spiritual standards in order to do this. Meetings can be made very interesting by fairly stating and meeting the questions of young people.

Where it seems advisable, the pastor should suggest, or still better lend, books on Christian living to his young people. Do not get any that are old and abstruse, written several generations ago, but something that is up-to-date. When young people have really been saved they will want to know how to live, and they will expect you to show them. They will believe you can back up all you say with the Word of God.

III. HELP THEM

Young people of today face a great many problems. Not finding the right solution for them causes many of them to go wrong. Excellent books have been published dealing with this subject. The pastor should own one or more of such books, and help his young people to get them.

One of the first problems of a young Christian usually is about what kind of amusements it is lawful for him to enjoy. He has unsaved friends, some of whom are professing Christians, who say there is nothing wrong with the theater, the dance, games of chance, etc. Unless he comes from a Christian background, he will want to know whether or not they are right. When talking to such a person, be sure of your facts. Do not denounce anything wholesale unless you know what you are talking about. Amusements are a form of worldliness and he who is a friend of the world is the enemy of God (James 4:4). Point out that anything that cannot be done for the glory of God should not be practiced by a child of God. Tell the inquiring Christian to pray about it and do as he feels God would have him do. If the seeker is honest, this will settle his problem.

When young people are about to graduate from high school, they face the problem of what to do after that. On the farm the solution used to be simple. The young fellow would help his father until he married and then settle down on a farm himself. The girl would help with the housework until she had a home of her own. It is not so simple today. For many the question is whether they should seek higher education and, if so, along what line. In most cases we would advise a young person to go to college. There are exceptional cases where this would not be wise—for instance, if the young person shows no interest in anything beyond his present sphere.

Along with this comes the problem of the choice of a vocation. Be sure you show an interest in the one who tells you about his dreams of the future. If you think he has any ability along the line of Christian service it might be that you could guide him into some form of it. Otherwise, point out to the one who asks you the strong and the weak points of the profession he prefers and pray with him about it. To see you take such an interest in his future will cause him to have respect for your judgment.

Perhaps the most important, as well as the most perplexing, problem is that of sex and marriage. God created two sexes for the perpetuation of the race. In order that this might be done properly and in order, He established marriage. In the days of adolescence both boys and girls begin to think about sex. In our day it even begins earlier because the movies and television shows put an emphasis on sex. It used to be said that if sexual instruction were given in time the coming generation would abstain from sexual sins. Time has shown that this is not true. Young people know more about sex today than any previous generation. Yet sexual sins among them are constantly increasing. In times past nothing was said about this from the pulpit, but the time is here when plain speech is necessary. The great importance of clean living should be emphasized by the pastor. To us it seems a good idea for the pastor and his wife to get the young people together once a year for a frank talk about sex. The pastor should take the fellows, and his wife, or some other capable woman, the girls. Sometimes it is well to get specialists to talk to them. In this way they will receive real help and many will be kept from falling into sin.

It should also be pointed out that marriage should be contracted only between Christians and Christians. This *can* often be pointed out in sermons.

The help we have suggested here can mostly be given through counseling and prayer. Happy is the pastor whose young people have confidence in him with their problems.

IV. SHARE WITH THEM

Every pastor should take a genuine interest in what his young people are doing. For a young minister this should not be difficult, for many of their interests are his also. There is, however, the danger of a young pastor in his first charge taking himself so seriously and considering himself so much above those in the church who are of his age, or a little below, as to drive them away. They may not literally leave the church, but his chance to influence them is gone. Every proper activity of his young people should be the pastor's concern. If they engage in any that are improper, he should in kindness seek to warn them of their dangers. Officiousness will be resented. Some will dare to do just the opposite of what the pastor told them. Where such practices are common, it will take time and much patience to overcome them.

The pastor should share in the social affairs of his young people. There was a time when the church was the social center of the community. That is hardly true any more, even in a small town. In many places the lodge or the high school takes that place. Where this is the case, it will not be easy to bring about a change. As far as the school is concerned, many principals will be glad to meet with the pastor and plan the social program so there will be no conflicts.

We believe the pastor has a right to attend every gathering of members of his church, be they old or young. If he is unable to attend the whole party or meeting, he should at least drop in for a few minutes and thus show his interest. The pastor's behavior at a party was discussed earlier (chapter 7). We say again that he should share in everything he possibly can.

Young people of high school and college age are usually interested in athletics. This is witnessed by their large attendance at baseball and football games. As long as they are in school, they will be rooters for the home team. It will be well for the pastor to share their enthusiasm. This becomes even more interesting when some of his own young people are on the team. We knew a pastor who traveled many miles to attend games in which the young people of his church were interested. If there are enough in your group, it might be helpful to initiate a team of your own for your church or Sunday school. But unless you are an athlete, leave the work of organizing in more capable hands. However, the pastor should always occupy a supervisory position and see to it that the language and behavior of his team are proper.

Sometimes amateur plays can be given by the young people of a church. Care should be used in the selection of the play to make sure it does not present a view or views contrary to the teaching of the church. We have a copy of a play about Judas Iscariot in which the betrayer of the Lord Jesus is portrayed as having done so with the best of intentions, for the purpose of forcing Jesus to assert His Messiahship and to seize the rule over His people by power. That is contrary to what the Scriptures teach about this "son of perdition" (John 17:12). Other plays may have other weak points. Participation in a wholesome play will help prevent young people from going to that which is questionable.

The pastor should be interested in the intellectual development of his young people. It is somewhat discouraging at the time school opens in the fall to find a number of students leaving for college. They are usually the finest and the best leaders. Of course, the wise pastor will do all he can to encourage them. If they have confidence in him, they will have counseled with him in the selection of their college. Unless they go to a church school that is true to the Christian faith, it is well to advise them to attend a school that has a chapter of the Inter-Varsity Christian Fellowship. This interdenominational organization is reaching into state universities and many other secular institutions of learning. It serves to bind together Christian young people and to help them mutually strengthen each other in the Christian faith. Before the students leave for college, have a farewell party for them in the church, in which you assure them of the good wishes and the prayers of the church. After they have gone, keep in touch with them by correspondence. We remember a young woman who complained quite bitterly that she had not received a single letter from her pastor while in college. She envied her friends who received frequent communications. Needless to say, she did not feel a great loyalty for that pastor.

There should also be a personal interest in each young person. This cannot be overemphasized. Without being officious, get as near to each one as you can. They like to have a pastor to whom they can look up, but be sure you do not assume an air of superiority. Do not meddle with strictly private affairs, unless the spiritual life is affected, and then talk with them kindly and understandingly.

The future of the church lies with the young people. If you can hold them, you will have gained a great victory.

Chapter 17

THE PASTOR AND THE ORDINANCES

We prefer to use the word "ordinances" rather than "sacraments." The word "sacrament" seems to imply some actual merit in its observance. This is definitely the view of the Roman Catholic Church and the Eastern churches. They recognize seven sacraments: namely, baptism, confirmation, the Eucharist, penance, extreme unction, holy orders, and matrimony. Some Protestant churches also use the term "sacraments," but with no thought of actual merit attached to them. To keep from any misunderstanding about them, we prefer to use the word "ordinances."

There are just two ordinances, according to the New Testament: baptism and the Lord's Supper. A few of the smaller denominations also consider feet-washing as an ordinance (John 13:14, 15). Most Protestants, however, consider the words of Jesus to refer to His example in humility.

Generally speaking, all Protestant churches practice the two ordinances, but not all. A few have renounced baptism as out of order in the present dispensation but still observe the Lord's Supper. Some have done away with both. Some claim that they are to be observed only spiritually.

Those who observe them do so in obedience to the command of Christ. The command to baptize is included in the Great Commission (Matthew 28:18-20). Jesus commanded the apostles to baptize new believers in the name of the triune God. The command to observe the Lord's Supper was given at the time of its institution. Jesus said concerning it: "This do in rememberance of me" (Luke 22:19). We believe the observance of both is in order today.

The form used in either or both of these ordinances may vary from denomination to denomination but the meaning is the same. Some have the communicants come and kneel at the altar in order to be served. Some have the participants remain in their pews but stand while the elements are being served. Some remain seated throughout the service. There are also differences in the mode of baptism used.

I. BAPTISM

According to our view, there is but one scriptural mode of baptism, which is immersion. However, we are very willing to say that we believe there are hundreds of thousands of believers in heaven in spite of the fact that they were baptized by affusion.

There is some difference of opinion as to who should be baptized. Pedobaptists believe baptism is to be administered to believers and also to their children. Others believe that only believers are to be baptized, according to the Scriptures. The emphasis is always put upon faith. Insofar as it is possible, the pastor who administers baptism should be convinced of the candidate's faith in Christ.

In order to determine this, it will be necessary to examine the candidate. In some churches it is deemed sufficient if the pastor has interviewed the candidate and is satisfied that he has been born again. In other churches, the Board of Deacons or Elders examine the candidate. Each member of the Board has the privilege of asking any question. If the Board agrees that the candidate is truly a believer, it brings a recommendation to the church to the effect that he be baptized. This custom is followed in many churches. In the church in which the author was brought up, each candidate had to appear before the whole congregation and in simple words give an account of his experience of salvation. Any church member could ask questions after this testimony. Perhaps since we grew up with it, this seems to be the most thorough method of examination. It always brought rich blessing to the church, and also to the candidate. In any case, the vote of the church decides whether a candidate is to be accepted for baptism or not. Through many years we have witnessed the examination of a great many candidates, and only on one occasion was one rejected. It was thought his account of conversion was too superficial. He was advised to make sure of his salvation and then apply again, so he was not rejected but deferred. But to the best of my knowledge he never came again.

Unless baptisms are very frequent, it is always well to bring a message on the meaning and significance of the ordinance. Some pastors bring the message before the baptismal service, and some have the baptism first. There is no hard and fast rule. If you have frequent baptisms, the sermon could be on any other subject.

Where baptism is by affusion, no special physical preparation is necessary. But where the candidates are to be immersed, extreme care should be used to provide for the safety and convenience of the persons baptized. The candidates in their baptismal robes should not be visible to the audience until they are in the water. Some of the older churches have very awkwardly located baptistries. The steps leading into the water should be safe. There should be enough water. If some of the candidates are taller than the pastor and the water is only waist deep, it requires quite an effort to perform immersion gracefully. The water should be of a moderate temperature. Great care should be taken to protect the modesty of women as they come out of the water. If the baptistry is so located that they cannot be seen outside the water, nothing further is necessary. But if they are exposed at all, have a deaconness stand at the head of the steps and throw a shawl or blanket over each woman candidate. Also, have a deaconness supervise their robing and disrobing.

The administering of the act of baptism is not difficult, though it may seem so to the pastor who is to do it for the first time. It is wise to have a short meeting with the candidates just before the service in which you assure them that all will be well if they do what you tell them and have absolute confidence in you. I once baptized a woman who weighed more than 300 pounds. Even in the baptistry she asked me if I was sure I could do it. I reassured her and all went well. Others are afraid you will let them slip. They do not stop to think that the water will bear the weight of the body. If properly administered, the ceremony is beautiful.

Do not permit a spirit of levity in the audience. In a small town often a lot of outsiders come out of curiosity to see baptism by immersion. Some are rude enough to make unbecoming remarks. We have even known Christians who talked about the pastor's attempt to "drown" them. In such a case we reminded them that this ordinance is just as sacred as the Lord's Supper, and we have never seen a real Christian who thought that the Communion was an occasion for the cracking of jokes. As a matter of fact, both typify the death of the Lord Jesus Christ.

II. THE LORD'S SUPPER

This is the ordinance that constantly reminds of Christ's sacrifice for our sins. In the broken bread we are asked to see His broken body. In the cup we are asked to see the reflection of His precious blood that was shed for us. The world may lightly esteem this, but for the child of God it is a service fraught with blessing. It is a memorial service always reminding us of the price that was paid for our redemption.

The meal also suggests the believer's spiritual nourishment, for as we partake of these elements they become symbols of that which sustains the flesh. Bread and wine were common items of food and drink in the land where Jesus lived and died. Jesus had declared Himself to be the Bread of Life that came down from heaven, and that he who ate of it would live forever. He had also said that unless men drank His blood they would have no life in them (John 6:51, 53). Of course this was not to be taken literally but spiritually. And in the Communion this is done symbolically.

As among the Jews the Day of Atonement was the most solemn observance, so it is among Christians with the Lord's Supper. It is not a sad occasion, nor is it one to be taken lightly. No spirit of levity should ever be present. The apostle Paul pronounces judgment upon the one who partakes of it unworthily (i. e., in an unworthy manner). It is always a blessing to the Christian who participates in a spirit of reverence.

There is a difference of opinion as to how often the Communion should be observed. Some believers do it every Lord's Day. Some observe it monthly, some bi-monthly, some quarterly, and some annually. The Scriptures do not make any specification. They simply say, "As oft as ye do it". We believe the annual observance is not often enough. Beyond this we offer no suggestions.

We do not know why but commonly the Lord's Supper is observed at the close of a morning service on the Lord's Day. It would seem more fitting to have it in the evening since it is a "supper." But here likewise we have no definite instructions in the Word of God. Circumstances may help to determine the time that is best suited to the majority in the congregation. We have known churches to observe it morning and evening of the same day since a goodly number of the members could not attend both services.

The elements originally used were bread and wine. The bread was the unleavened bread used at the Jewish Passover. We believe it is desirable to use the same kind of bread if it is obtainable. In the city *matzos* (unleavened bread) can always be bought in the Jewish market. In a small town this may not be possible. In such a case we believe there is no reason why ordinary bread should not be used. Quite certainly the wine used was lightly fermented, for such was in common use. Some insist upon using fermented wine today, but this is not necessary. Since sweet grape juice is obtainable, this is to be preferred, for it satisfies the symbol of representing the red blood of Christ. We note in passing that in connection with the Communion it is always called the "cup" and never "wine."

The order of procedure is quite clearly indicated in the Word of God, except for certain details. We offer these suggestions to the young pastor who is presiding over a Communion service for the first time, for usually this is done by the pastor. However, in some churches the service is conducted entirely by the deacons.

The Communion is usually observed at the close of the service, either morning or evening. While an appropriate hymn is sung after the sermon, the deacons come forward. In some churches they occupy the front pews; in some they face the audience. The pastor sits behind the table with half of the deacons on either side of him. The table has been arranged before the service and is covered with a white cloth. After all have been seated, the pastor or one or two of the deacons remove the cloth, folds it, and lays it aside. Then the pastor stands and reads a passage from the Scriptures setting forth the institution and meaning of the service. We have found it well to read from Matthew, Mark, Luke, or I Corinthians 11, taking one selection at each service. Some pastors prefer to give a brief meditation setting forth the great facts symbolized by the service.

As Jesus offered prayer before serving the elements, so do we also. Separate prayer of thanksgiving is offered for each of the elements. This can be done by the pastor, but we believe it is better if at least one of the deacons is asked to pray over one of the elements. It keeps the service from becoming too formal.

The bread is always served first. It is well if a piece of the bread has been left unbroken so the pastor can break it before giving the plates to the deacons. Then the deacons proceed down the aisles and distribute the bread. In some churches the participant eats the bread as soon as it has been served; in others each waits until all have been served, then they partake together. Make clear which custom you intend to follow. In practically all churches individual cups are now being used, for they are more sanitary than the common cup of former years. After the cups have passed, all partake at the same time. If there are no receptacles for the cups, the deacons will collect them after participation.

In some churches it is customary to serve the pastor first; in others he is served last. The order is immaterial. The pastor himself serves the deacons after they have returned from serving the congregation.

When the cups have been regathered, or, if they are not regathered, when all have partaken of the cup, the white cloth is spread over the table again and the service brought to a close.

It is customary to have some music or singing while the people are being served. Either the organist plays appropriate hymns, or the choir or congregation joins in singing well-known numbers. All this helps to make it a deeply devotional service. If there is sufficient time, some pastors like to conclude with a brief testimony meeting. Often there is a fellowship offering after the Communion, which is used for the relief of the poor. Make sure that no one thinks this is in payment for the meal.

After Jesus had instituted the Lord's Supper we read: "And when they had sung an hymn, they went out into the Mount of Olives" (Matthew 26:30). This suggests the proper way to close a communion service. Use a hymn or a chorus that can be sung without opening any books. If this is done, a benediction is not necessary. The pastor's "Amen" dismisses the service.

CHAPTER 18

THE PASTOR AND FUNERALS

In addition to the regular meetings on Sunday and the mid-week prayer meeting, the pastor will be called upon for some special services. These will include the performing of wedding ceremonies, the conducting of funerals, and the celebration of special occasions. In most of the Pastor's handbooks we have seen, weddings are mentioned first and then funerals. This may create the impression that a funeral is next in order after a wedding, which of course is not true. Furthermore, a new pastor is more likely to have a funeral before he has a wedding. It is for these reasons that we reverse the order in this book.

All special services will require special preparation. This is true of funerals, weddings, and any other special observances and celebrations. It is possible that the young pastor has not attended many such services, or if he has been present, has not paid much attention to the procedure. In any case, he may have given no thought to the preparation that goes into such services. It is for this reason that we discuss them somewhat in detail in this book.

Death is no respecter of persons and funerals will have to be conducted for all kinds of people. In one case the service will be for one who has lived to a ripe maturity; in another, it will be for a young man or a young woman. Even young children are taken by death. For each of these an appropriate service is to be conducted. Sometimes the departed will have been known as a saint and remembered for all sorts of kindnesses he performed; sometimes he will be a person with whom it was very hard to get along, a fact well known in the community. In some instances death will have come after a long illness; sometimes very suddenly and unexpectedly. It may even be the pastor's lot to conduct a service for one who was murdered, or for one who has committed suicide. Because he is a minister of the Gospel, he will be expected to adapt himself to all circumstances and to do and say that which is appropriate.

I. BEFORE THE SERVICE

If death has occurred in the home of one of his members, the pastor should make it his business to visit the home just as soon as possible. He should not go to the homes of members of other churches except by invitation, or at least until after he is sure all arrangements for the funeral have been made, lest he create the impression that he is trying to take charge of another's responsibility. Where the people in the home did not belong to any church, he has a right to go and to see if he can be of any service.

Such a call in the home of mourning should have as its aim to bring some degree of comfort and also to help in making arrangements for the funeral service. The occasion provides a wonderful opportunity for showing sympathy and ministering the comfort which comes from the God of all comfort. Often the mourners are dazed and do not know what to do. It may be the first death in the home and they do not know the first step to take.

To such people it will mean much if the pastor sits down with them and quietly offers helpful suggestions about the time, the place, and the program. The time should be suitable to both the pastor and the mortician. Either one may have another previous engagement for that day and hour. The place today is commonly the funeral parlor in the city, but in the small town the church is still commonly used. Sometimes the service is conducted from the home. In the matter of the program, it is best to respect the wishes of the family if it is possible to do so. Occasionally they will have no plan and leave it all to the minister. Where it is desired that a former pastor or another minister should have a part, this wish should by all means be granted. As far as music is concerned, some pastors prefer organ music only, and no singing. We feel that it is well to ask the family if the deceased had any favorite hymn, or if the family has any, and then help select a soloist, or a duet or trio, to sing at the service. This will mean more than just the music of a familiar hymn. Sometimes they will have people in mind to serve as pall bearers; sometimes they will depend on the pastor for suggestions. In some cases they will need help in sending messages to relatives and friends who live at a distance. Offers to help in these and any other necessary matter will usually be appreciated.

Sunday funerals should be avoided if possible. They are an extra strain on the pastor and as a rule could easily be held on the day before or the day after.

It is a beautiful custom to have many flowers at a funeral, but it is unwise to spend a great deal of money on flowers that will be laid on the grave only to wilt or to freeze. Frequently today those who wish to give flowers are directed to send money instead which will be used for some worthy project, sometimes in the name of the deceased. The project might be something for the church, or something for missions. If any counsel in this matter is desired, the pastor should be prepared to give it.

II. AT THE SERVICE

If the funeral is from a home or from the funeral parlor, the body will already be there, but if it is in a church it will be brought there only for the service. The pastor should be there about ten minutes before the service is to start. He need not speak to the mourners but should let them know he is there. If it is a church funeral, the pastor will precede the coffin as it is being carried up the aisle. Usually soft organ music is played while the body is brought in. The pastor proceeds to the pulpit and the service begins. We submit an order of service that we have found very useful.

Organ Music
Introductory Statement (can be an appropriate verse of
    Scripture)
Scripture and Prayer
Vocal Music (solo, duet, trio)
Message
Vocal Music
Prayer and Benediction

It used to be the custom to read the obituary of the deceased, but that has been discontinued for some time. Great care should be taken in the preparation of the funeral message. In some places there is a trend to do away with the sermon and to substitute a liturgy. Liturgical churches of course do not need the sermon, but we believe there is a place for it in other churches. The message should not be longer than about fifteen minutes. It should be directed to the living, for the lot of the deceased will not be affected by it. Its aim should be to bring peace and comfort. If the deceased has been known to be a sincere Christian, this should be mentioned. If there is any doubt about it, or if he was not a professing Christian, it is best to avoid any personal remarks. Do not get the reputation of "preaching everyone into heaven." Bring out the main facts of the Gospel and advise the mourners to find their comfort in God. I once conducted a funeral for a suicide, and used for a text Psalm 55:22: "Cast thy burden upon the Lord, and he shall sustain thee." Burdens such as sin, sickness, and sorrow were mentioned. Not a word was said about the deceased.

If the departed belongs to a lodge, the family may desire a lodge funeral. In such a case, it seems wise to have the fraternity conduct its service first and then let the pastor take over. The occasion may never arise, as it never did in twenty-six years of pastoral work in my experience.

It used to be customary to say at the conclusion of the message that the service would be concluded at the grave. Present day custom closes the service in the church with a prayer and benediction, for many will not go to the cemetery.

When the coffin is being taken from the church, the pastor precedes it to the hearse, and again at the cemetery he precedes it to the grave. The service at the grave should be brief. It should consist of a brief passage of Scripture especially pointing forward to the resurrection, followed by the committal and prayer and benediction. Some use the Lord's Prayer, which does not seem to be quite in order here. There are pastors who object to the committal which says, "Earth to earth, ashes to ashes, dust to dust" because it is too abrupt a change from the message of comfort to a hole in the ground. But it is Scriptural and we see no objection to it. We prefer to drop flowers on the coffin instead of dirt. If you use the commonly accepted committal, be careful to eliminate unscriptural statements from it, such as that of the "general resurrection." After the benediction shake hands with the principal mourners and quietly assure them of your prayers for them. The funeral party leaves the cemetery before the coffin is lowered into the grave.

III. AFTER THE SERVICE

The house of mourning should be visited a few days after the funeral. If it is a church family, the visit will be greatly appreciated. Sometimes the time may be profitably spent by recalling incidents out of the life of the deceased, but be careful not to tear open wounds which are just beginning to heal.

Make sure that the mourners do not get the impression you have come to collect a fee. Make it a point never to expect a fee from members of your church. Conducting funerals is a part of your pastoral ministry. However, if a gift is pressed upon you, it is sometimes wiser to accept than to offend. If the family had no connection with the church, it is a different matter. You have given of your time and effort and it is only proper that some reimbursement should be given. However, if none is offered be sure you do not create the impression that you expected one.

If there are unsaved members in the family, the follow-up work may enable you to win them for Christ, especially if the deceased was a Christian. If he was not, then call attention to the importance of being ready to meet God at any time.

CHAPTER 19

THE PASTOR AND WEDDINGS

This is also one of the special services the pastor will have to conduct, sometimes shortly after he becomes a pastor.

It is customary today to speak of the entire marriage ceremony as the "wedding," but properly speaking the word "wedding" belongs only to the ring ceremony. Strictly speaking, a marriage service without the ring ceremony is not a wedding. There was a time when the ring ceremony was not used by many Protestants. Today most non-liturgical churches have no objections to it. It is in reality a beautiful and symbolic act.

There was a time when the minister or the church was the sole judge as to who might be married. It was customary to proclaim "the banns," the intention of the two to get married, some time in advance, so that if there should be any objections or reasons why they should not be married, this might be stated and evaluated beforehand. In our day the laws of the state have something to say about it, making marriage both a civil and a religious institution. Couples who do not want to come under any obligation to a minister or a church have only the legal ceremony, performed by a judge or a justice of the peace. Since marriage is controlled by the state, the minister should make sure he knows the law of the state in which he is to officiate. In most places he is required to be an ordained minister, but in many places it is sufficient if he is pastor of a church and authorized to perform all the functions of a pastor.

I. BEFORE THE CEREMONY

It should be remembered that the pastor is under no obligations to marry every couple that comes to him with a marriage license. No state will force a minister to marry a couple against his will. The license is an authorization for him to do so if he is willing. If he has any compunctions about officiating, he may not escape responsibility by saying that if he does not perform that ceremony some other minister will.

Most denominations have regulations governing the conduct

of their ministers, but perhaps the principal situation in which the matter becomes acute is in the remarriage of divorced persons. Some pastors seem to think that if the state has granted a license there is no reason to refuse to officiate. Others take the position that under no consideration will they officiate if one of the parties has been divorced. If this is your conscientious conviction, we advise you to stand by it. We believe, however, that it makes a difference on what grounds the divorce has been obtained. If the pastor is convinced that this is the "innocent party," he may officiate. But in such a case he must be sure of the facts. Totally strange parties who have been divorced are better turned away.

The minister should not hesitate to give the reason why he refuses to officiate. If the rules of his denomination forbid it, he may give this as his reason. If it is against his own principles and a matter of conscience with him, he should not be afraid to say so. But it should be done courteously and kindly.

Another questionable practice is the marrying of a believer and an unbeliever. Pre-marital counseling will enable the minister to discover where the couple stands spiritually. Some refuse to officiate unless they have been able to counsel with the couple first. We believe it unscriptural to unite a believer and an unbeliever. In almost every case that has come under our observation, it is the believer who loses out. The risk is too great. However, it may be possible to bring the unbeliever to Christ during pre-marital counseling. In just one instance over a period of twenty-six years of pastoral work, I felt compelled to marry a couple where the groom was a Christian and the bride was not. But in just a few months the bride had also accepted Christ and a Christian home was founded.

The minister should be informed in good time that his services will be desired at a coming marriage. This will avoid the embarrassment of having a conflicting appointment and the necessity of calling on another minister the last minute. Usually the couple comes in person to the minister to make this request, but if the groom comes from another community it is perfectly proper for the bride to make the arrangements.

One more point the pastor should remember before he performs the ceremony is that of the marriage license. He should request to see it before he officiates to make sure that everything is in order. If the parties are well known to the minister, he need not be as careful as he must be when he faces perfect strangers.

The other details of the wedding are usually arranged by the family of the bride, though in some cases the pastor is called on for advice, for he is supposed to be fully informed about the etiquette of a marriage service. It is a good thing for him to have authoritative information in hand.

II. THE CEREMONY

There is little difference between a church wedding and a home wedding where the church is small. Possibly the church wedding is a little more formal. The church of the bride is considered the proper place for the wedding, even if she expects to join that of her husband afterwards. But even here exceptions are permissible.

The ushers are supposed to see to it that the room is in order for the ceremony: candles, flowers, white carpet, etc. The bridesmaids will put the last finishing touches on their costumes and that of the bride. The minister, the groom, and the best man are in a side room awaiting the opening chord of the wedding march. There is usually an organ prelude and possibly a vocal solo. After the bride's mother has been seated, the doors are thrown open and the march begins. The minister walks slowly to take his place within the chancel facing the audience. At short intervals he is followed by the groom and the best man. They stand at his left, half turned, watching for the entrance of the bride. When the bride arrives on the arm of her father, the groom usually steps forward to take her from her father's arm, and both take their places before the minister. From time immemorial it has been the custom for the man to stand on the right of the woman and the woman on the left of the man. This means that the woman is on the right of the minister and the man to his left as he faces the couple. When the groom has received the bride from the father, the father steps back and remains standing until he has "given" his daughter to be married. The bridesmaids and groomsmen "close in" slightly, and the ceremony begins.

Most ministers have their own manuals, handbooks, or rituals directing them in the proper conduct of the ceremony. In a nonliturgical church it is well to consult with the bride as to which ceremony she prefers, for some are longer and some shorter. For a long service, the full Episcopal marriage ceremony may be used. Shorter forms have been prepared by other ministers. We believe it lends dignity and authority to a ceremony if the pastor has his book in hand even if he has memorized the whole ceremony. When addressing the couple, it is best to use the given name by which they are commonly known instead of the full names which appear on the license. After both have said their "I do," the minister asks,

"Who giveth this woman to be married to this man?" The father answers, "I do," or "Her mother and I do." Then he takes his seat by his wife's side.

And now the real marriage begins. The couple is asked to join their right hands and often the minister keeps his right hand upon theirs lightly. Then the pastor administers the vows, addressing the man first and then the woman. The vows are repeated phrase by phrase. It is best to use short phrases rather than long ones. Sometimes a devoted Christian couple has memorized the vows, and this makes the ceremony especially beautiful. If the ring ceremony is used, it will follow immediately after the vows have been spoken. The best man hands the ring to the pastor, who hands it to the groom and directs him to place it upon the third finger of the bride's left hand. While thus holding the ring, the pastor again outlines the words the man must say. If it is a double ring ceremony, he also takes a pledge from the bride according to the ceremony he is using.

The wedding prayer follows, which we believe is better if extemporaneous rather than read from a book. After the prayer, there is a symbolic joining of the hands again. Many at this point prefer to clasp together the joined hands of the couple and to say, "Those whom God hath joined together, let no man put asunder." After this he will declare the couple to be husband and wife. For the final blessing some prefer to have the couple kneel upon cushions before the minister. When the ceremony is finished, it is now customary to have the new husband kiss his new wife. Then congratulations are in order. However if there is to be a reception immediately after, it is customary to have the recessional, after which the couple will stand in some convenient place to receive congratulations.

III. After the Ceremony

There is not much more to be done by the minister. He must fill out the license and get witnesses to sign it. He should make sure that the completed license is put in the mail at the proper time.

If the couple comes from his church, or at least one of the parties, the pastor usually remains for the reception. If they are total strangers, it is not out of order for him to withdraw after the ceremony.

It has long been the custom that the honorarium given to the pastor is by him passed on to his wife, though there is no rule about this.

We append here an "evangelistic" ceremony which we have

used when we knew unconverted friends would be present at a wedding. After reading Ephesians 5:17-33 and a brief prayer, the ceremony begins.

Dearly Beloved:

The ordinance of marriage had its beginning with God. God saw in the Garden of Eden that it was not good for man to be alone, and so He made him an "help meet for him." He brought the woman to the man and gave her to him, and the man accepted her from God's hand as his wife. Thus was set the pattern for the human relationship of marriage. It is an appointment of God and therefore is to be entered into soberly and discreetly, as in His sight.

It should be remembered also that in the marriage service there is a pictorial representation of the union of a human soul to Christ in salvation. As the bridegroom has wooed the bride until she gave her consent, so the Holy Spirit has wooed the soul until He obtained the answer "Yes." And as in this public ceremony the bride and the groom will publicly declare and confess their love for each other and pledge their faithfulness each to the other, not with fear or shame, but with joy, so the soul that has come to Christ will make an open confession of love and faithfulness to Him with boldness and joy. At the same time, it is an act of faith in both cases. The parties to be married will take each other's word, and believe it with all the heart; and so will the soul that comes to Christ.

Now the same Word of God that teaches the way of salvation will also give you the counsel and instruction you will need in your new relationship to each other. And remember, the union to be established between you today is not to be broken by any power save that of death.

In token therefore of having chosen each other as partners for life, you may join your right hands.

(Then the minister says to the man:)

Do you, *Charles,* take *Elizabeth,* whom you now hold by the right hand, to be your lawful and wedded wife? Do you promise to love, honor, cherish, and protect her; forsaking all others, in sickness as well as in health, in adversity as well as in prosperity; to cleave only unto her as long as you both shall live? If so, answer, "I do."

(The minister says to the woman:)

Do you, *Elizabeth,* take *Charles,* whom you hold by the right hand, to be your lawful and wedded husband? Do you promise to love, honor, and cherish him; forsaking all others, in adversity as well as in prosperity, in sickness as well as in health; to cleave only unto him as long as you both shall live? If so, answer, "I do."

(Then shall the minister say:)

Who gives this woman to be married to this man?

(Answer by the father or someone else appointed to do so:) I do.

Is there a ring? (Loosen hands)

(The pastor, taking the ring from the best man, hands it to the groom and says: Repeat after me:)

With this ring I thee wed; with my heart's faithful affection and my worldly goods I thee endow, in the Name of the Father, the Son, and the Holy Ghost.

(Repeat the same words for the bride in a double ring ceremony).

The union now formed is to continue as long as you both shall live, and it is important to call to mind the duties you have solemnly assumed. Put God first in your lives and in your home, then you will be able to weather the difficult and stormy days as well as the bright and cheerful ones. Do not neglect prayer and the reading of God's Word.

You, the new husband, have the duty of providing for the support of the new wife, to shelter her from danger, to cherish for her a manly and unchanging affection, and to love her even as Christ loved the church and gave His life for her.

And you, the new wife, are to reverence your husband, to be submissive to him, and to put on the ornament of a meek and quiet spirit which is, in God's sight, of great price.

It is the duty of both to be submissive to each other and to delight in the society of each other, not only today but in the long years that stretch ahead; to remember that in interest, reputation, and affection, you are henceforth one and undivided; to preserve an inviolable fidelity and to see to it that what God hath joined together, no man shall ever put asunder.

And now by the authority vested in me by the laws of this State as a minister of Jesus Christ, I pronounce you husband and wife.

Prayer and Benediction.

CHAPTER 20

THE PASTOR AND NEW MEMBERS

If a church is to grow, or even to survive, it will be necessary to add new members from time to time. Many pedobaptists recruit their new members from the babies they have baptized. Those who do not practice infant baptism have no such "resources" and need to use a different method.

On the Day of Pentecost there were only 120 believers in the morning; before nightfall three thousand more had been added to their number. The addition of members does not always occur as rapidly as that. This was also true of the Jerusalem church. Later we read that the Lord added to the church daily those that were being saved (Acts 1:16, 2:41, 47 ASV). This shows that sometimes they come in large numbers and sometimes one by one. There is no reason to become discouraged if the membership is not growing as fast as you would like to have it.

There are pastors who are anxious to build up a large membership, and to this end devote all their efforts, while others think it is more important to see souls genuinely saved than to have names on the church roll.

I. ENCOURAGEMENTS TO MEMBERSHIP

There are a good many people who are Christians but who do not have membership in a local church. They are members of the Lord's universal Church by virtue of the fact that by the Holy Spirit they have been baptized into the Body of Christ (I Corinthians 12:13), but we believe it is also important for them to have membership in a local church. Perhaps all they need is some encouragement to cast in their lot with the local church.

Such encouragement may be given by a public invitation. A general statement to the effect that those who are interested should speak to the pastor or one of the deacons is sufficient for some. They may have attended the church for quite a while and have begun to wonder whether or not the pastor is interested in having them come in as members. All they need is such an invitation.

148

Some pastors "open the doors of the church" once a month and encourage prospective members to come forward.

A word of caution is necessary at this point. It is always preferable if the candidates come voluntarily. Then they can never say that they were "talked into joining the church." It shows greater conviction and interest if they apply as volunteers.

In some cases it may be necessary to make personal calls on prospects. Some people will come to church all the years of their life and never apply for membership, even if publicly urged to do so. They are waiting for someone to call upon them personally. It is sometimes best to let the deacons or other church officers do the soliciting. Too many people think it is just a professional matter if the pastor does it. He does it only because it is his job. We have heard of the pastor of a small church who built up a large membership by going from house to house in town and community and urging people to join his church. If people told him they could not attend services, he told them that did not matter just so he had permission to add their names to the church roll. He brought a wonderful report to the conference and as a result was given a much larger church, which of course had been his ambition.

We believe it is well for a pastor to let Christian people who attend his services know that their membership would be desirable, but always make sure that people will not take you for a "head hunter," but realize that you have their best interests at heart.

II. CANDIDATES FOR MEMBERSHIP

Some candidates for membership come as a result of an evangelistic campaign in your church or in your community. If the meetings were held in your church you should regard it as your duty to establish contact with all converts as soon as possible. Since they were saved in your church, it is reasonable to believe that from the human standpoint at least your church has the first claim upon them for membership. Converts will usually acknowledge this. The church in which they were saved is like a spiritual mother to them. They feel at home among its people. The pastor will show his interest in their spiritual welfare by calling on them and praying with them. It will be easy to mention the church and the blessing of having fellowship with it.

If it has been a union campaign, every pastor has the right to call upon all the converts, unless there has been a definite expression of preference for another church.

The pastor should make as sure as it is possible that those to whom he speaks have actually been born again. There are too many unconverted people in our churches today, and in most cases they are the trouble-makers. A deacon once told a young pastor: "Remember, the people you receive as members into the church are the people you will have to work with." This is sound advice.

Other candidates are Christian people who attend the services but are not members. Usually there are some such in most churches. Occasionally you will find some who are very loyal to you and to your church but who will never consent to become a member. They will do everything they can to help the church, sometimes even encourage others to become members, but as for themselves, they will never take the step. We knew an excellent Christian woman who was very regular in church attendance and always willing to help where she could. She was a fine Bible teacher for young people and for women's classes, but she refused to become a member and would not reveal why.

Then there are some who will gladly come in as church members, thinking that in so doing they become Christians. To such it should be made very clear that membership in a local church is valuable only if they have been born again. We have served several churches where we could have added many more members than we did but we felt that many of those who were interested gave no evidence of having been born again.

Do not grab anyone in sight as a prospective member. Let it be known that it means something to come into the church as a member. Make it clear that only those who have accepted Christ as Saviour by personal faith will be considered eligible for membership.

Some people become members by letters of transfer from other churches. If the letter is from a church of the same denomination, there is usually no question about the individual's qualification for membership. However, it is not obligatory to receive anyone without investigation, even from churches of the same denomination. Some churches honor letters from other denominations; some require an account of Christian experience from such candidates.

III. PREPARATION FOR MEMBERSHIP

This applies particularly to new converts. Some may never have been to church before and have no conception as to what it means to belong to a local church. Even some who are more or less acquainted with the church may need instruction. The pastor should form a class to give instruction to such incoming members. It is wise to organize such a class shortly after the close of an evangelistic campaign. The class should not be too formal, and the prospective church members should be given opportunity to ask questions about things they do not understand.

The instruction given should be at least along four lines:

(1) The essentials of Christian doctrine, especially what it means to be saved. The preaching from the pulpit is helpful in this respect, but these great truths can be made much plainer to a small group and to individuals.

(2) The importance of Christian living. This is very necessary, for in our day many church members make no difference between their lives and the lives of those who are not Christians. New converts should be taught from the epistles of the New Testament just what is expected of the Christian, what things he ought no longer to do, and what things he ought to do. Do not be afraid of "too much negative," for the Bible emphasizes negatives as well as positives.

(3) The constitutional requirements of your particular church. We have found churches where no one could lay hands on the constitution when the new pastor desired to see it. The constitution acquaints the new member with the structure of the church and also specifies what is expected of the church members.

(4) The incoming members should also be taught the importance of supporting the Lord's work. In some European countries there is a state church supported by the government. But even here the "free" churches depend upon their membership for the maintenance of their work. For this reason the new member should be shown what it costs to maintain a church and the fact that the church counts on all its members to contribute all the money it takes to keep it in operation. Be sure you also point out the importance of giving for missions. A live church will be interested in helping to make the Gospel known everywhere in the world.

Before being received as members of the church, candidates should be carefully examined, even after receiving a course of instruction in church membership. The object of the examination is to help make sure that the candidate actually has spiritual life and that he understands what it means to belong to the church.

Some think it sufficient if the pastor has a personal interview with each candidate and, if he is satisfied, there is nothing in the way of receiving the applicant as a member. Most churches have the prospective members meet with the Board of Deacons or the Board of Elders and be examined by them. Each board member has the right to ask any questions he may consider important. If the board is satisfied, it should report to the church a recommendation that the candidates examined be admitted to membership in the church. In a few churches the candidate is expected to give an account of his Christian experience before the whole church. This can be a great blessing to the candidate and also to the church. Sometimes this testimony is deferred to the day of the public reception into the church.

IV. THE TIME OF RECEPTION

This should not be deferred too long with new converts. If the pastor does not believe in personal solicitation, he should at least announce publicly that if any of the new converts wish to come into the church they should get in touch with him or with one of the deacons. If nothing is said or done, the new convert may easily think that no one cares about whether he comes into the church or not, and he may easily slide back into the former way of life.

It has already been mentioned that some pastors "open the doors of the church" once a month at which time they ask those who are interested in membership to indicate their desire by coming forward.

Easter is considered by many an ideal time to receive new members into the church. There is nothing in the Scriptures to support this. As a matter of fact, it was on the Day of Pentecost rather than Easter that the first large addition to the church in Jerusalem was made. However, we think Easter is a good time because the church is usually filled with people on that day. Many are present who do not go to church on ordinary Sundays. It is worth something to have them see who is coming into the church.

There is no hard and fast rule as to the time of receiving new members. It can be done on any Sunday that is convenient. It does seem appropriate to do it in connection with the observance of the Lord's Supper, unless this is done only once a year. A prospective member might even lose interest if his actual reception is deferred for three months, if the Communion is observed only quarterly.

V. THE METHOD OF RECEPTION

In denominational churches there is usually a prescribed procedure which can be found in the ritual, manual, or handbook. The method here suggested has been used with satisfactory results in more or less independent churches.

Before the Communion service, the Chairman of the Board (Deacons or Elders) presents the names of those on whom the Board has passed and recommends them for reception. Upon motion the church then votes to receive them. As a rule there is no question about receiving them. However, if anything serious should have been found in the conduct of any candidate that would disqualify him for membership, it should be mentioned at this time. Mostly this is a form, like the challenge at a wedding to mention anything that should keep the parties from becoming married or to "forever hold his peace." Then the deacons come forward and stand in front. The candidates are asked to come forward and stand facing the deacons, or occupy the front seats. If the candidates are to testify, it is best to have them sit and take their turns at testifying. After this there should be brief remarks by the pastor on the significance of church membership. BUT DO NOT PREACH A LONG SERMON! After this the right hand of fellowship should be extended by the pastor, followed by the board members. If the church has a church covenant, this should be read at this time by the church and the new members. Prayer by the pastor or someone appointed by him should be offered for the new members. The final act should be the signing of the church constitution. The old members should be encouraged to welcome the newcomers into the church. If the church is small enough, it is possible to have the new members stand in front while the members of the church pass by and shake hands with them.

All this will take considerable time, but if it is done on a Communion Sunday the pastor may not want to give a long Communion meditation anyway. But keep in mind that the more impressive you make the reception of members the more it will mean to the new member.

Chapter 21

ORGANIZING A NEW CHURCH

Unless a man is employed by a denomination or some other organization to establish churches in unchurched areas, the chances are that he will not organize more than one new church in a lifetime. Many will never have that privilege but will always step into works that are already established. There is a peculiar blessing in being the pioneer in the founding of a new work. The man who undertakes to do so must have some definite leadership qualities. And he must have boundless courage and not give up in spite of all kinds of opposition. He should have a strong conviction that the Lord wants him to do this work.

If it is to be a denominational church, counsel should be sought from a denominational adviser. Possibly the denomination has a man whose work is that of organizing new churches. What is said here has to do with independent or congregationally governed churches.

I. The Need of a New Organization

Sometimes churches are located where there is no special need. A small town which could be served by three or four churches sometimes has seven or eight. But there are also many unchurched areas.

1. *A church split.* Our first word here is that a split should be avoided if at all possible. If there is a division in the church over an issue, or over an individual, every effort should be made to heal the breach and to keep the church together. It will give both the pastor and the church a bad name if there is a split. It is certain that some bitter feelings will always be left. In conversation with a pastor whose church had been in operation for a good many years, we made the remark that we were glad our church had not come into existence as the result of a split but that people from a number of churches had found this a central place where a work for the Lord could be started. The pastor answered that his church had resulted from a split and that some bitterness still existed in spite of the fact that many years had passed.

Sometimes there are good reasons why a split cannot be avoided. We know of several churches where the pastor thought there was opposition against him and feared that this opposition would grow until he would be asked to resign from the pastorate. To forestall this, he proceeded to read the names of people who would no longer be considered members of the church. In the one case, the members thus expelled were a group large enough to get together and form a new organization.

Sometimes there is doctrinal corruption which has crept in and divided the membership. Usually the pastor is the leader of one group while the other group has its own leader from among the members. If the evil cannot be corrected, it may be the wisest thing for the two groups to separate.

In some churches there is so much worldliness that it is impossible to carry on a spiritual ministry. Unless this is overcome by a revival, a separation may seem necessary. Sometimes an overwhelming majority of the members belong to a secret society and they dominate the church. One pastor told us that he had so many lodge members in his church that the community nicknamed it the temple of that lodge.

There are also splits that are made for the benefit of the work. A church has grown so large that it is deemed advisable to divide it into two congregations with an amicable spirit. In one place a large number of members came from the neighboring small town. A peaceful agreement was reached by which those of the neighboring town and vicinity should withdraw and form a new congregation. Some large churches establish branches and when the branches are strong enough to go on alone, they are allowed to form a separate organization. We believe this to be a wise procedure. It is a mistake for the mother church to try to keep all its branches under its control.

2. *A new community.* Every city has many unchurched communities, especially on the outskirts. Stores and theaters usually keep up with such developments but it is common for the churches to lag far behind. In country communities and in small towns there is often room for the forming of a new church. Many small churches have been closed in this auto age. People say they prefer to go a little farther and attend a larger church in the city. The trouble is that many end up, not going to church at all. In such places, the church building is still there but is not being used. And yet there are enough people who could be interested in getting the church started again.

Often the first step is the organization of a branch Sunday

school to meet on Sunday afternoon. Usually there are enough people even in a small church who want something to do and would be willing to teach a class. It is never hard to round up enough children who would go to Sunday school if they could. The children will come if the parents will let them. Sometimes it is much more difficult to convince the parents than the children of the desirability of having a Sunday school in the neighborhood.

After the Sunday school is in operation, it is possible to arrange for a week-night preaching service. The attendance may be small in the beginning and it will take a lot of calling to get interest stirred up. It will take much courage and patience to start a work in a new community. Possibly a short series of evangelistic meetings can be arranged before long.

If there is no abandoned church available, often the use of the school house can be secured. If not, then a vacant store building may be available. If there is nothing else, the work may be started in a home, that of the pastor or of someone else in the community who is interested.

II. How to Proceed

To start from scratch in a new community a lot of calling will be necessary. Let the pastor do all the calling in the beginning until he knows the people of the community fairly well. Most likely he will find a few families — maybe only one — that is interested. He should secure the help of these in calling and stirring up interest. It will help if the people of the community see that some of their own neighbors are interested in the project.

After the community has been thoroughly canvassed, it is time to call for a general meeting. Call in all the homes again and tell the people of the meeting, extending a cordial invitation to all to be present. A good many will not come. If the meeting is too small, decide with those present to hold another one in the very near future.

If you are organizing a denominational church, the denomination will doubtless be glad to send someone from headquarters to supervise the organization. If the church is independent or congregational in government, you will be able to work out your own program.

The meeting should open with a prayer by the leader or with a season of prayer. However, the season of prayer might wait until the project has been outlined. This should be done by the leader, or by someone from the community who is respected and who is capable of making a good presentation. The advantages of having an organized church in the community should be made plain — such as bringing the Christians together for a united testimony. Then time should be given for questions. The variety of questions may be great and the leader should be prepared to answer them all. When the discussion has ended, a clerk should be appointed to take the minutes of the further procedure. A motion to organize will be in order and this should be acted upon according to parliamentary rules. This is the very first stage.

Then it will be in order to appoint several committees. One of these is to draw up a constitution. Suggestions should be received as to what name to give to the new church. Another, committee should be appointed together with the pastor (who is leading in the establishing of the new church) to draw up a statement of faith. This could be made a part of the constitution. Some churches also like to have a church covenant which is to be read before a Communion service and also at the reception of new members.

Before dismissing, arrange for a subsequent meeting at which the proposed constitution, doctrinal statement, and the covenant are to be considered and, if satisfactory, to be adopted. Do not defer the next meeting too long. Keep striking while the iron is hot.

The next meeting should be the organizational meeting. Of course it should begin with prayer. If possible, the proposed constitution, statement of faith, and covenant should have been mimeographed so that a copy can be given to each one present. The next period should be devoted to the reading and discussion of the proposed documents. There should be a very frank discussion and all questions should be answered. It may be that the majority will like a little more time to think the matter over. Do not let the time for decision be postponed too long. The documents may be voted on separately, or section by section, as the congregation prefers. When they have been adopted, the new church has a beginning.

If there is sufficient time, elect the first church officers. If not, decide on another meeting when this will be done. The officers elected should include the following: pastor, clerk, financial secretary, church treasurer, missionary treasurer, Sunday school superintendent, some trustees, and a board of deacons. Then you are ready to move forward. It will be well not to have too complicated an organization at the beginning of a new work. It can be expanded as the church grows in numbers.

In all probability there will have been Sunday school and preaching services some time before the organization was effected. The time has now come for the organization to function. It is best to set aside a morning service on some Sunday not too far in the future for an "Induction service" at which the newly elected officers will be installed and the work of organization begun.

The program should be carefully planned by the pastor. If possible there should be several special musical numbers, although the most important part of the meeting is the induction of the officers and the inauguration of the work of the new church.

It is quite possible that there will be an air of excitement, but the pastor should do his best to bring about a quiet, devotional spirit. If God is to be glorified by the service, it should be carried on in a spirit of reverence, no matter in what kind of building the service is held.

After several hymns, Scripture reading, and prayer, there should follow the signing of the constitution. This should have been placed on a desk near the pulpit. If the constitution is in a book, there should be plenty of space for all the signatures. This should also be done if it is a separate document. The pastor should sign first, then the officers in order, and then the members. Those signing on Induction Day will constitute the charter members of the church.

After the signing of the constitution, it is time for a brief address by the pastor pointing out the significance of the step that has been taken and outlining the duties of the officers. If there have been temporary officers before and temporary records kept, these should now be turned over to the new officers. Then the officers should be asked to stand before the pulpit while the pastor offers a special prayer for them.

The service should close by all the officers and members forming a circle and joining hands to sing "Blest Be the Tie That Binds." After this the pastor should pronounce the benediction and dismiss the meeting. Thus will end the first meeting of the newly organized church.

We are of the opinion that the more impressive you make this service the more it will mean to those who come in as charter members, and the greater will be the impression made upon those who have not come in as members.

If it is Scriptural to have local churches, it is certainly Scriptural to have membership in a local church. From the legal standpoint it is important to be incorporated, and this also makes a constituency necessary. Get a Christian lawyer, if possible, to help you with the incorporation so your church will have legal standing.

But always remember that organization and incorporation will not insure the success of the church. There must be much hard work and rich blessings from God in answer to prayer.

Chapter 22

BUILDING A NEW CHURCH

There were many organized churches in the days of the New Testament, but as far as we know there were no separate church buildings. The apostle Paul usually began work in a new place by preaching in a Jewish synagogue. When he was cast out of the synagogue, he sought another place where the work could be continued. In the city of Corinth he went into the house of a man named Justus which was next to the synagogue (Acts 18:7). In Ephesus he secured the use of a lecture hall of a man named Tyrannus (Acts 19:9). In the epistle to Philemon we discover that the Colossian church met in his house (Philemon 1:2). This seems to have been the general custom. Just when Christians began to build separate church buildings we do not know for certain. It may not have been before the days of Constantine when Christianity was first recognized as a legal religion.

As we saw in the previous chapter, even today churches may begin in a home or in a rented building. In Catholic countries of Europe we have seen small Protestant groups meet in the missionary's home.

But if a church functions properly and grows, it will become necessary to find better housing for it. Besides, with the many activities centering in a church, a separate building becomes a necessity.

I. Reasons for Erecting a New Building

We mention some of the most important reasons:

Sometimes it is a newly organized church that needs housing. It may have begun in a home or in a school house or in a rented building, but after a while it becomes evident that a more suitable building is needed.

In some cases it may be an old church that has been in the same building for many years, but the building has become inadequate for present needs. It may date from the time when all the church wanted was an auditorium in which to hold the Sunday meetings. Or it may be a two-room building with a sanctuary and a "lecture room" (whatever that was supposed to signify). Usually the wall between it and the sanctuary was removable so that the two rooms could be made into one for a large meeting. There was no office or study for the pastor and no separate rooms for Sunday school classes. It is felt that a better work could be done in a more modern building.

However, we sound a note of warning here. Sometimes pastors get the idea that if they had a nice, new building, crowds of new people would come to their services. It usually does not work that way. Much work has to be put into a calling program to get people to come.

Another reason for the erection of a new building is found when a church is outgrowing its old place of worship. The sanctuary is filled for every meeting. This is a healthy sign. It shows that the church is alive and growing. This is possibly the best reason for deciding to erect a new building. It is embarrassing when strangers come and cannot find seats. Usually they will not come a second time. So it is time to build a new church.

II. How to Start

Most likely there will have been unofficial talk about it among the people for some time. This is a good way to arouse interest. The more people talk about it, the more they will become interested.

The pastor's first move is to discuss the matter with his official board. This may be done at one of its regular meetings, or a meeting specially called for the purpose. It is better to discuss it with the board first than to have a general meeting at once. Too many ideas will come to the surface at a general meeting. Talk it over thoroughly with the board and secure their unanimous backing. It will be hard to get the idea across to the church if there is a minority group that is opposed to the plan.

When the board is agreed, it is time to bring the matter before the whole church. It may first be mentioned at a regular business meeting and then plans made for a general meeting at which to reach a decision. At this meeting the board should bring its recommendation before the church and make sure that the church knows that the board is unanimous. There may be some difficulties to overcome. There may be a few who are opposed to the plan. Or, as we saw it happen once, someone recommended that the example of another church be followed which had abandoned its building program and decided to give the money for missions instead. Such people need to be won over.

When the church has acted favorably on the recommendation, there should be some discussion about the type of building to be erected. Of course details cannot be worked out as yet, but there should be some decision about the size of the building, the type of architecture, and also the approximate cost your congregation can afford. Too often far too expensive buildings are erected, and sometimes buildings that are too large.

A building committee should be appointed to work out the details. Remember, the pastor is *ex officio* member of the committee and should always meet with it, but he should not be the chairman. He should make sure the members of the building committee understand clearly what he thinks ought to be done, but leave it to them to make the final decision. This of course means that he must have a clear idea of what he thinks would be most suitable. He may get his ideas by looking at other churches. He should defend his ideas, but not become offended if the committee does not adopt all his suggestions.

The building committee should employ an architect and tell him what kind of church building they have in mind and have him draw up plans. When they are satisfied, the plan should be submitted to the church for adoption. Some alterations may seem necessary. But the church should come to a unanimous decision.

The building committee should look after all the details. Sometimes the pastor interferes too much, and makes a terrible mess of things. As a rule he is not a builder himself. In one place we knew, the pastor had planned the building, with the result that there was a room in the basement that did not have any window. In another place where the pastor had planned the building, the ceilings were too high and the wooden wall between the sanctuary and the lecture room served as a perfect sounding board for an echo so that it was very difficult to preach. In still another instance the pastor drew the plans for the new building and supervised its construction. An adequate building resulted. But during the months of the building the congregation had to endure poorly prepared sermons. So the best procedure is to let an architect draw up the plans.

III. How to Raise the Money

Building has become very expensive. Very often the first estimate given by a contractor proves to be far too low. More has to be added to bring the building to completion. A good financial program should be planned to take care of the cost.

The first attempts at money-raising should be made long before you start building. This can be done in various ways. Often small banks are given to every home, including the children in the Sunday school. Frequently each child wants a bank of his own. Both children and adults should be encouraged to put something into the bank as often as they can. At a regular time these banks should be brought to the church and opened, perhaps every month, or every quarter. We believe every month is better, for in three months interest may die out. After each collection, the total should be reported, and also how much there is in the fund now.

In addition to this there should be a monthly building fund offering in both church and Sunday school. By and by you will have a nest egg to begin with.

When you have fully decided that you will build, it is time to find out how much cash can be raised by your congregation. By this time you should have your architects' plans and an approximate idea of the amount you will need. In addition to this, it is usually necessary to have people sign pledges payable in from one to three years. Where there is a good congregation, some well-to-do members, and people who are liberal givers, this may be sufficient to raise the entire amount. It is best if this can be done.

But if anything is lacking, it will have to be borrowed. It is quite difficult to borrow money from a bank for a church building. Churches have been found to be poor risks. Often church loans have to be refinanced at a loss to the bank. As a result, some banks will not lend to churches at all. We know of two big city churches that have heavy debts hanging over them. In the case of one, the community has completely changed and the church is thinking of moving. In the other, the church has a downtown location and has been there for many years. It is a large and beautiful church but it seems unable to get rid of its debt. Private individuals are the best sources from which to borrow. Some churches float a bond issue.

When you have borrowed money, see to it that payments are made on time and earn a good name for your church. We know of a church where a new pastor found that the coal bill of the previous year had not been paid. When he tried to find out how much it was, the coal dealer told him to forget about it — he was used to that. But the pastor insisted that his church would pay, and he saw to it that it did. It gained a much better reputation for the church in the community. Thus it will be if your building debt is paid on time.

IV. WHAT TYPE OF BUILDING

The type of building you erect depends on several things. The size of the congregation has something to do with it. So does the community and the size of the town in which you are locating.

There is also the matter of taste. Years ago some churches built very plain buildings. Later some very elaborate models were produced. The present trend is to be very modern. It will be impossible to please everybody, but there should be a general agreement by the congregation. We offer a few suggestions.

The church, especially if it is a small church, should be *attractive but not gaudy.* You want it to look like a church.

It should be *pleasing but not too costly.* We have already indicated how some church debts drag on and on. Jesus was born in a lowly place and some think that this suggests that our church buildings should be very humble. But if we live in modern and attractive houses, the Lord's work should be carried on in a building that is not inferior. We were in a community once where the people lived in very up-to-date homes but worshipped in a very old-fashioned church building. This seems out of order.

The church building should be *substantial and not temporary.* A tabernacle type of structure, if erected, should be only intended for a brief period of time — likewise if the church builds only a basement to begin with. This is sometimes done if there is not enough money in sight to complete the building. This may serve the purpose for the time being, but be sure you *do not stay in the basement* longer than absolutely necessary. It creates a bad impression on the community to see a congregation meeting in a basement church for six, eight, or even ten years.

Sometimes, especially in a small town, many members will be willing to donate labor. They may not be able to give much money but they have time to give to the construction of the building. In such a case they should be given credit according to the current wage scale.

Occasionally a church has a good carpenter or contractor in its membership who can do a good job in erecting the building. Do not expect him to donate his services. If there is none in your church, engage one from elsewhere. It may be he will be the only one you will have to pay. This will be a great saving to the church.

It used to be said that when a pastor has completed building a new church, it is time for him to resign. Possibly this was due to the fact that arguments and dissensions had arisen about certain details in the building, and these had resulted in ill feelings. This should not be necessary, if the leadership has been wise.

The psalmist may have had a residence in mind when he wrote these words, but we feel they apply to the building of a church: "Except the Lord build the house, they labor in vain that build it" (Psalm 127:1).

Chapter 23

THE PASTOR AND CHURCH DISCIPLINE

The matter of church discipline is a subject that is greatly or totally neglected by a great many churches. It seems there is a desire to keep the membership list as large as possible no matter how some of the members behave. There are churches that revise their membership list occasionally — sometimes every year — but it is mostly on the basis of whether the members attend the services or at least contribute something to the support of the church. If they still come once in a while, or if they give or send a small sum of money every year, they are left alone.

In the Old Testament there were strict laws to deal with those who violated the commandments of God. In the New Testament we are not under the Law, but this is no reason why inconsistent behavior of a member should not be dealt with. The New Testament teaches church discipline. The Lord Jesus did not found any local church, but He outlined the method of procedure when one brother had transgressed against another (Matthew 18:15-19). The apostle Paul founded many local churches and in his epistles he gives rules for their government. He is very definite in pointing out in some cases what should be done with certain offenders (I Timothy 6:3-5; I Corinthians 5:13).

We believe the church that does not practice any discipline is not an obedient church and cannot expect the fulness of the blessing of God. Besides, it will get a bad name in a community if it is known that some people who live evil lives are still church members in good standing.

I. THE MEANING OF DISCIPLINE

The term has been used to designate the method of government of a local or denominational church. But that is not what we have in mind here.

There is a positive and a negative side to the subject. Perhaps we should say that one side deals with instruction of how members ought to behave and the other with instructions on how to proceed if they do not behave.

Let us look at a few of the definitions given by the dictionary. One is, "teaching and instruction." This is what it should mean principally in the home. Children should be taught what is right and what is expected of them. This is bringing them up "in the nurture and admonition of the Lord" (Ephesians 6:4). This also applies to church members. Just as a newborn babe has a great many things to learn in this world, so the babe in Christ needs a great deal of positive teaching. He needs to have a grasp of the doctrines of the Bible, and he also needs to be instructed in Christian living. The Lord once said, "My people are destroyed for lack of knowledge" (Hosea 4:6). The same is true of many church members. They have not been trained in Christian living and it should not seem strange if they fail.

The other side of "discipline" means to chasten, to punish when the conduct has not been right. Parents do it in the home; teachers do it in school; and it should also be done in the church of God. Dobbins says: "From this basic idea of instruction and training has come the derived meaning of correction and punishment." It is with this thought that we wish to consider it here. And it is this thought, possibly, that frightens many churches away from it.

II. WHEN IS CHURCH DISCIPLINE NECESSARY?

The New Testament mentions four classes over whom discipline ought to be exercised.

1. *Broken fellowship and an unforgiving spirit* (Matthew 18: 15-17). The disciples had been disputing among themselves as to who should be the greatest in the kingdom. It is in this connection that Jesus speaks of one brother transgressing against another. A spirit of self-exaltation will always result in broken fellowship. We have known of church members who were not on speaking terms with each other, although they still attended the same church. Sometimes the offense is of another nature. Dishonesty in a business deal will also serve to break fellowship between Christians. Still other things could be mentioned. Whenever fellowship has been broken, something should be done to restore it.

In the same connection we have the teaching of Jesus about forgiveness. Peter wished to know how often he was obliged to forgive a brother who sinned against him. He thought there was a limit to forgiveness. When Jesus told Peter he should forgive "seventy times seven" times, He undoubtedly meant one should never stop as long as there was any sign of repentance. This condition may also exist among church members. They attend the same services, sometimes partake of the same Communion, but there is enmity in their hearts against each other. This should not be allowed to go on.

2. *Unbelief and doctrinal error.* Paul says, "Mark them which cause divisions and offences contrary to the doctrine which ye have learned; and avoid them" (Romans 16:17). It does happen that church members take up a strange doctrine and still wish to remain in the church. If they are left alone, they will seek to subvert others. For this reason they should be dealt with. Paul said, "Avoid them." How can this be better done than by removing them from membership if they remain obstinate and continue in the way of error?

In his first epistle to Timothy, Paul makes mention of Hymenaeus and Alexander who concerning the faith had "made shipwreck" (I Timothy 1:19). Evidently there had been a gross departure from the Christian faith as Paul preached it. What Paul says about "delivering them up to Satan" corresponds with what he wrote to the Corinthian church about an offender of a different kind (I Corinthians 5:3-5). Since in that case he means they should put the offender out of the church, we believe that is what he means here too.

Paul also speaks of those whose doctrine is not according to godliness, who teach contrary to the wholesome words of the Lord Jesus Christ, who engage in disputings with corrupt minds, and he advises Timothy: "From such withdraw thyself" (I Timothy 6:3-5).

We believe where discipline is exercised at all, churches are more inclined to deal with a member who has fallen into open sin than one who has fallen into false doctrine. Yet the latter is far more dangerous than the former. A departure from the teaching of the Word of God as interpreted by the church should not be tolerated.

3. *Trouble-making resulting from a disorderly walk as a Christian.* It may mean the fomenting of strife, or it may mean stirring up envy and jealousy. Sometimes it is manifested in greediness and selfishness. There are some who constantly carry tales and gossip about one church member to another. Sometimes the whole church eventually becomes involved if the evil is not nipped in the bud. We have known of at least one church that split in two as a result of a lot of gossip.

Again, we have known churches who took a strict stand against the use of intoxicating drink and tobacco. If any member was known to be guilty of either or both of these, he was called before the church, and if he did not apologize and ask forgiveness his name was removed from membership. We do not criticize this, but in the same church the members of a family might be quarreling about an inheritance and nothing was done about it. By no means do we condone drinking and smoking, but in our estimation quarreling about an estate among believers is far worse.

4. *Open wickedness and immorality.* Such was the case in Corinth (I Corinthians 5). The same nature of immorality will hardly be found today, although it is by no means impossible. But in our day, when sex is so openly flaunted, it is not at all strange that some are drawn away by the lust of the flesh. Such cases usually become known to the community, and if the church does nothing about them, it lowers respect for that particular church. Wickedness may be manifested in other ways, such as drunkenness and dishonesty, and in each case should be dealt with.

III. THE ADMINISTRATION OF DISCIPLINE

Who should administer church discipline? We believe it should not be initiated by the pastor. If he is aware of the sinning of a member, we believe his first responsibility should be an attempt to set that member right again (Galatians 6:1). This is a very delicate task. Only a spiritually minded pastor can do it. He should try to get the offender to see the greatness of the evil he has committed and show him the way back by confession (I John 1:9). This can be done without anyone else in the church knowing about it. The pastor's aim should always be to help an erring member. But this cannot go on forever. Dr. Strong says, "The Church is not a Mutual Insurance Company, whose object is to protect and shield its individual members" (*Systematic Theology* by A. H. Strong, p. 925). He goes on to say, "It is a society whose end is to represent Christ in the world, and to establish His truth and righteousness."

It is best if such cases are brought before the church by a deacon or some other member. The pastor is more like a judge than a prosecuting attorney. We know of churches where everything is brought before the whole congregation for disposition. We believe this is a serious mistake. It makes the sin far too public. When an offense has been reported to the pastor, it should be investigated at once. This can be done by the Board of Deacons or a special committee appointed by the Board. In small churches the deacons headed by the pastor sometimes do this work. We believe it is wiser if the pastor is not on the committee. It will shield him from false accusations. The committee should meet with the member and thoroughly investigate the charges brought against him. If they are true, he should be urged to confess and ask forgiveness. If he does this, the matter is settled, except that the committee reports to the church that the case has been closed. The details need not be aired before the whole congregation. If it is a sin against another member, both should be visited and great care taken to find out on whose side the fault lies. Then they should be urged to become reconciled. And if this is done, it should be reported to the church. Many members could be saved for the Christian life if they were thus dealt with.

It may happen that an offender is anxious to escape judgment, and immediately asks to be forgiven without any show of repentance. If nothing is done to him, he will most likely go on and commit the same sin again. The truly penitent may ask the church to exclude him from membership, so that it may free itself from the charge of condoning wickedness. He will accept it with humility, continue to attend the services, and in due time seek and receive restoration. The church should always be willing to forgive one who repents.

However, if there is a stubborn spirit, an unwillingness to repent, there must eventually follow exclusion. Jesus outlines the procedure. If someone sins against you, go and talk to him privately. If possible, become reconciled again. If your attempt is not successful, take one or two others along with you and try again. If this also fails, bring it before the whole church. And if he does not obey the church, consider him "as an heathen man and a publican."

We believe there should be two stages in the exclusion. The first should be temporary with the hope that the sinning member will repent and come back. Earnest prayer should be offered to this end. If there is no repentance, the name should be removed from the membership list.

The exclusion should be public so the whole community will know of the action of the church. It will usually have a wholesome effect.

The aim of pastor and church should always be to bring the offender back to fellowship. We have known some excluded members who immediately went into deep sin, making it impossible for Christians to have fellowship with them. But even then they should be remembered in prayer.

With this we close these simple directives to the young pastor who is serving his first church. Much more could have been added, but we deem this will be sufficient to help the beginner. We know the book is incomplete. Our opinions may not always be the right ones. But we have earnestly endeavored to support our position with the Word of God whenever we found it possible. We trust that it will be a help and a blessing.

INDEX

INDEX OF SCRIPTURE REFERENCES